Andrea's Journey

Andrea's Journey
FROM FREEDOM FIGHTER TO TRUE LIBERATION

ANDREA JACOB

ANDREA'S JOURNEY
FROM FREEDOM FIGHTER TO TRUE LIBERATION

Copyright © 2024 Andrea Jacob.

All rights reserved. No part of this book may be used or reproduced by any means, graphic, electronic, or mechanical, including photocopying, recording, taping or by any information storage retrieval system without the written permission of the author except in the case of brief quotations embodied in critical articles and reviews.

iUniverse books may be ordered through booksellers or by contacting:

iUniverse
1663 Liberty Drive
Bloomington, IN 47403
www.iuniverse.com
844-349-9409

Because of the dynamic nature of the Internet, any web addresses or links contained in this book may have changed since publication and may no longer be valid. The views expressed in this work are solely those of the author and do not necessarily reflect the views of the publisher, and the publisher hereby disclaims any responsibility for them.

Any people depicted in stock imagery provided by Getty Images are models, and such images are being used for illustrative purposes only. Certain stock imagery © Getty Images.

ISBN: 978-1-6632-4063-7 (sc)
ISBN: 978-1-6632-4065-1 (hc)
ISBN: 978-1-6632-4064-4 (e)

Library of Congress Control Number: 2024901963

Print information available on the last page.

iUniverse rev. date: 08/16/2024

To
my mother;
those who fought and died;
the survivors;
the many who awaited this book before their passing;
anyone who feels lost and may need a testimony
to envision how God can change their life;
people interested in knowing the truth about the events
that took place around the time discussed herein;
my children and loved ones who may not
understand the path my life took;
the honest of heart; and
all those who believe in the true liberation of humankind.

CONTENTS

Acknowledgments ix

Chapter 1	Early Years.. 1
Chapter 2	Awakening 15
Chapter 3	1970 Revolution... 25
Chapter 4	Introduction to "the Organization" 33
Chapter 5	Commitment.. 41
Chapter 6	Urban Guerrilla 47
Chapter 7	Bank Robbery... 53
Chapter 8	On the Run 63
Chapter 9	Interrogation.. 73
Chapter 10	Trial and Sentencing 83
Chapter 11	Prison Life.. 89
Chapter 12	Conversion 103
Chapter 13	NUFF Speaks from Prison 111
Chapter 14	Postprison... 119

The Answer.. 141
Epilogue 143
Appendix.. 145

ACKNOWLEDGMENTS

I wish to extend my heartfelt gratitude to those individuals without whose help I would not have been able to complete this autobiography.

First, I would like to thank God, from whom all blessings flow and with whom all things are possible, for granting me the strength, courage, wisdom, and determination to persevere with this venture.

Second, I wish to thank some special people who have contributed steadfastly and urged me on throughout the entire exercise.

I refer to Bhagi, Jaiye, Slinger, and Conci, who selflessly parted with their treasured collections of newspaper clippings and other paraphernalia to facilitate this production.

I also want to acknowledge calypsonian Winston "Gypsy" Peters and my friends Lionel Remy and Patricia Ison, who encouraged me and supported me every step of the way, as well as all the others, including the numerous calypsonians, playwrights, poets, and writers who highlighted the cause by educating the people and supporting the struggle—and those who contributed in other ways, including all believers.

Finally, my typists Y'rusha, Denzyl, and Carlan James provided the technical assistance necessary to make this book a reality.

1

EARLY YEARS

"Stop!"
"Get down!"
"Don't move, or we'll shoot!"
"Hands in the air!"
"Shoot up the house!"

These were the orders being barked by heavily armed policemen. After jumping five or six feet to the ground from a kitchen without steps, I had just landed. A few minutes earlier, at about five o'clock in the morning, I had been aroused from sleep atop a bunk bed in the front bedroom of the flats I had been occupying for the past few weeks, by the sound of the engine of a heavy vehicle. Upon fully awakening, I realized that the vehicle had stopped in front of the house, the windows of which were almost level with the road.

Since this was a strange occurrence at that time of the day, I sat up on the bed, pulled the curtain back slightly, and peeped outside. I was horrified by the sight that I beheld. Less than thirty feet from where I was sitting was a bread van with a popular logo from which was emerging policemen armed to the teeth with self-loading rifles and submachine guns.

I frantically got out of bed, simultaneously waking the other occupant of the room, who was asleep on the bottom bed of the double-decker, by calling his name and exclaiming, "Police!" He got up and immediately took off like a bullet. I, on the other hand, desperately ran to a side window of the room, hoping to make my exit from there, only to discover that there was a line of similarly armed policemen along that side of the house.

My only recourse to avoid capture was to run for it through the kitchen door. After my unorthodox exit, I recognized that the house had been surrounded. I had jumped straight into the arms of the police. The van's occupants were the last set of policemen getting into position.

Looking around, I felt, *This is it!* I had been finally captured after four months on the run, with a ten-thousand-dollar bounty on my head. As always, whereas the average person would be experiencing great fear, I was not. A great calm seemed to come over me. I was scoping out my surroundings, still seeking a way of escape. I noticed the other occupant of the room was now in the custody of the police. Accepting that there was no escape this time, I complied, reluctantly raising my hands above my head while at the same time being ordered to get up slowly. I obeyed. All guns were then trained on me.

Advancing toward me was Mr. Randolph Burroughs, the head of the then Flying Squad, a specially trained group of police officers whose apparent role and function was to bring us in dead or alive. He placed his arm around my shoulder and said, "Jay, you are better than Malick. He was always ten steps ahead of the police, while you were always one."

Abdul Malick, a.k.a. Michael de Freitas, or Michael X as he was called, was a Trinidad and Tobago–born self-styled black revolutionary and civil rights activist of the 1960s who had recently been captured by the police after being sought for murder. Holding me by the hand, he led me in the direction of the road while giving orders to "shoot up the place." I began to plead with the police, explaining that there was a woman with a young baby in the house and that the other occupants were all innocent. They did not know my identity.

The police kept asking for Guy Harewood and Brian Jeffers, among others. Jasper and Jeff, as they were fondly called, were regarded as leaders of the organization known as the National United Freedom Fighters (NUFF). The police had had the house under surveillance and knew that there were visitors the day before but were unaware of their departure. After much pleading, I managed to persuade them.

My companion and I were then led to the street and made to face a wall with our hands held high up against it. Subsequently, we were placed in a vehicle. I reminded the police that they had disturbed my sleep and that I hadn't had my breakfast yet. They laughed, then got us biscuits and cheese and proceeded to the nearest police station, later taking us to the Criminal Investigation Department, Port of Spain.

On arrival there, Chipo, the other occupant of the house, and I were separated. I was escorted to a room where I was offered a chair, on which I was told to sit. Mr. Burroughs then left the room after promising to return. In the solitude of that room, reality began to set in. *How did I get to this place in my life?* I asked myself. *Is all this happening, or am I dreaming?* It was the first time that I had gone beyond the front desk of a police station. While seated alone in that room, I began to retrace the events of my life that had resulted in my then present situation.

EARLY YEARS

It all began on December 1, 1952, when in the southernmost part of an island in the West Indies called Trinidad, in a little oil town called Point Fortin, in Fanny Village, the sixth child was born to Nathaniel Jacob and Veronica Thomas. Mr. Jacob, or "Wise Man" as he was known to all, was a jack-of-all-trades: joiner, carpenter, farmer, and fisherman, among other things. Veronica worked as a cook and a maid for some of the English, Spanish, and Dutch and other expatriates who managed the Shell Oil Company and resided at Clifton Hill, Point Fortin.

Point Fortin was originally made up of three separately owned coconut estates, the employees of which lived in barracks provided by the owners. Trinidad Oilfields Limited discovered oil in Point Fortin in the early twentieth century. This led to the subsequent merging of the three estates and the beginning of industrial activities that centered around producing, refining, and marketing crude oil. The face of Point Fortin was now changing from agricultural to industrial. Increasingly, its economic development depended on the extension or curtailment of the company's operations or the benevolence of private individuals.

There was an increase in population since people from the neighboring Caribbean countries, Grenada, Carriacou, Saint Vincent, and Barbados being among them, sought employment in response to the demand for manpower. The growing township of Point Fortin became home to them, as well as to other expatriates who came from different parts of the world as the oil company expanded, developed, and changed ownership.

Neither parent, not even in his or her wildest dreams, had even the faintest idea of the events that were predestined to take place in the life of their child whom they named Andrea Lucina Jacob. My earliest recollection is from around the age of three. The house in which we lived was a wooden *ajoupa*-type house covered with carat leaves. The smoke from the fireside, which was used for cooking, resulted in the ceiling and other parts of the house being covered with black soot.

Our family at the time consisted of my mother, my father, three elder sisters, two brothers, and me. The furniture in our home was composed of a few wooden chairs, a table, and a bed. The children slept on bedding and a fiber mattress that was placed on the floor. On rainy nights we would all be awakened from sleep. I would be made to stand against the wall while my parents and siblings placed pots, buckets, pans, and other receptacles on the floor to catch the rainwater that leaked from the roof.

Although our upbringing was poor and humble, my father ensured there was always food in the house. This he did by cultivating dasheen, peas, cassava, corn, and other food crops.

My father owned a copper, which is a large round iron receptacle, on which he made cassava bread and farine, the latter to preserve the large quantities of cassava produced. He also made starch by grating the cassava, wringing it in a piece of cloth, and allowing the liquid to settle. The water was thrown away and the residue dried and used to make starch, which was used to smooth the cotton clothes worn at the time. Ironing was done with a coal pot and four irons heated on the coals.

When corn was reaped, the leftovers were partially husked, tied together in pairs, and strung over wooden rods placed overhead along the ceiling. These were left to dry and were later used for plants or were rehydrated by soaking them in hot water, grating them into cornmeal, and making dumplings, *paime, pastelle, coo coo*, porridge, and other delicacies. The smaller ears were dried and stored in barrels to be used as feed for the fowls and ducks that we raised. Almost all the poor families reared livestock and animals to augment their sparse incomes.

My favorite delicacy was chili bibi, which was made by parching the corn, grinding it in a mill, or pounding it in a wooden mortar with a pestle and adding sugar after sifting. The green corn was roasted or boiled with salt, coconut milk, and seasoning.

A horizontal plank was nailed against a coconut tree in the yard, and a vertical one supported it, which was about waist high. A sheet of zinc covered the former with projections on either side. Another plank was attached horizontally to the tree about six inches above the vertical plank with the aid of another heavy plank. This apparatus was used to press sugarcane, the juice of which was boiled and used as a sweetener.

I remember my father giving purges made of senna leaves, Epsom salts, seawater, molasses, and lemon juice to the entire household. Returning to school following a school vacation without a purge was considered a capital offense in our household. This concoction would be given while it was still dark out. The family would be awakened and be made to stand in a wet place and drink a cup of this brew. Since there was only one latrine or outhouse, holes were dug in the garden behind the house for each of the children and covered with pieces of galvanized steel.

A large pot of yam "pap" porridge was prepared without milk, sugar, or salt and could be had as often as one desired throughout the day following the purge. The makeshift latrine holes were covered with dirt, and a few months later a sugarcane plant was planted in each of them.

My mother, the eldest child in her family, was forced to terminate her schooling when in standard 2 following her mother's death. She had to take care of her siblings. Her father, "Dada" as he was fondly called, was a landowner who owned a large portion of Salazar Trace, Point Fortin. My father's parents were also landowners at Matelot. Jacob Settlement in Santa Flora was named after his father, Charles Jacob. My father, however, died before the land was divided, so my mother and his children were deprived of their inheritance. Both my parents had roots in Carriacou, Grenada.

One of the highlights of this period of my life was when my mother worked overtime at the cocktail parties and other similar events held by her employers. Sleep was hard to come by on these nights, since the thought of the leftover delicacies that she would bring home kept us awake.

My mother would often tell of the children who were rude and spat on her, calling her "nigger" and by her first name. Since it was not customary for adults to be called by their first names, this was regarded as a form of disrespect. However, there were also the "madams," who sent used clothes, toys, various treats, and other items they no longer used to give to her children, especially at Christmastime.

I remember vaguely there was a quarrel while we children were in bed one night. There was talk about money and Lancer's dance. My father was angrily soliciting money from my mother so that he could attend this dance. My mother left that night, never to return to live with my father. She subsequently came for her children, whom she worked for and supported as best she could. My father died when I was age seven. I was probably too young to understand the full implications of these events. My two eldest sisters and brothers all went out to work to make ends meet, which involved assisting with paying rent, feeding the household, and sending the younger ones to school.

Above left: Andrea's father, Nathaniel Jacob, in the early 1960s.
Above right: Andrea's mother, Veronica, in the late 1940s.

I remember vividly my first introduction to formal education at Mrs. Mahadeo's private school, which began at three years old. My early elementary education was at Point Fortin ASJA Muslim School. While about 90 percent of the teachers were of East Indian descent, the majority of the students were of African descent.

Those days were happy ones. We read from *Nelson's West Indian Readers* and learned about Sir Francis Drake, Ralph Abercrombie, and John Hawkins, who were projected to us as heroes. Christopher Columbus, we were told, discovered Trinidad on his third voyage around the world and was honored for doing so by Queen Isabella and King Ferdinand of Spain.

We were taught in West Indian History that at the time of the discovery of Trinidad by Christopher Columbus in the year 1498, the native dwellers, that is, the warlike Caribs and the peaceful Arawaks, were the original inhabitants of the island. Africans were subsequently kidnapped, captured by warring tribes, and sold to traders, while others were enticed and spirited away to the West Indies via the slave trade to work on various sugar and cotton plantations. They were forced to endure the agony and pain of being separated from their loved ones and their homes. During the journey via the Middle Passage on ships that were unsanitary and overcrowded with little food and water, some died on the way, some threw themselves overboard, and others were beaten and placed in stocks for resisting. Only the strong survived.

On arrival in the West Indies, these African natives were auctioned off to the highest bidder, sectioned off, separated from their families and tribes, dehumanized, stripped of their freedom, religion, and identity, and not allowed to maintain their culture, including their African names. Family life was discouraged. They were made to adopt the names of their slave masters and were forced to toil on the land of these foreign countries. They lived under poor and inhumane conditions, performed hard labor, and because of poor nutrition were subject to diseases. They often had cruel masters and were frequently flogged and tortured. The slaves retaliated by burning plantations, running away or escaping to the hills, and sabotaging equipment, for which they were mercilessly flogged or sometimes put to death.

We were told that slavery started in 1606 when four hundred seventy Africans were brought to Trinidad by Dutch slaver Isaac Duverne. Slavery was abolished in 1833, after which former slaves served an apprenticeship period that ended on August 1, 1838, with full emancipation. Some of the freed slaves remained under their masters' roofs, while others stayed as far away from the plantation as possible. Chinese people were recruited to work the plantations in 1806 but were not suited for arduous labor in the blazing sun, so they resorted to becoming shopkeepers, small businessmen, merchants, and peddlers.

Indentured laborers were subsequently recruited from India, the first batch arriving on a ship called the *Fatal Razack* on May 30th, 1845. These laborers were made to work from sunrise to sunset and were paid very low wages, which enabled them to barely survive. They lived in barrack-type houses and were able to keep their religion and culture. When this final period of indentureship came to an end on January 1st, 1920, some stayed on the plantations, while others started their own farms but a minority returned to India.

The island changed hands on several occasions, being ruled by the Spanish and British, there came also the French settlers which is partly the cause of the cosmopolitan nature of our land. Each of these colonizers and settlers left their mark in the form of varying aspects of their culture. This is evident in the languages, architecture, and music, among other things, including the names they gave to towns and streets.

I grew up in a mixed community where some of my closest friends were of East Indian descent. There was the Chinese shop where my mom did part-time work. I spent considerable time with my neighbor Ms. Dolly, an East Indian woman. It was there that I learned to *leepay* or plaster the dirt floor and walls using *gobar* or cow dung; make sada roti; and make my own chulha or fireside, which was all part of East Indian culture.

One of my favorite pastimes with Ms. Dolly's nieces was

imitating an Indian wedding. We would dress up in makeshift saris and *ohrinis* and sing East Indian songs. Among my favorite songs were "Dil Di Ki Dey Ko," "Bhugi Laago Vin," and "Boloji Boloji."

Among my school friends were Myrna, Cynthia, Brenda, and Judy. We would frequent the *gri-gri* and guava patches and climb the mango and *pommerac* trees after school, relishing the fruits that we found there. We played hopscotch, three A, Hula-Hoop, and skip before and during the lunch period and also after school.

There were also the moonlit nights when most of the neighbors and their children would assemble around a bonfire to roast corn or suck sugarcane. The elders would tell folktales about Papa Bois, *douens*, La Diablesse, *soucouyants*, and the boo-boo man, which scared the living daylights out of some of us, causing us to huddle together to sleep and also serving to keep many of us from going outdoors late at night. There were no streetlights in our area at that time; we had to rely on the light of the moon and stars. At times the children would play ring games such as Fine Castle, Drop Peter Drop, Farmer in the Dell, and London Bridge.

At school, we learned Irish songs, Scottish songs, and other songs from around the world, including "Old Kentucky Home," "Loch Lomond," "Auld Lang Syne," and "Old Black Joe." These were truly enjoyable times. During the vacation, I would spend hours at the nearby beach, with neighbors and friends catching crabs and sea cockroaches or just playing and bathing.

August 31, 1962, was designated as Independence Day. This holiday replaced British Empire Day. The queen of England no longer ruled Trinidad and Tobago. We now had our own national anthem, flag, pledge, emblem, and coat of arms. We also sang our national songs, which included "Our Land of Sun and Seas," "God Bless Our Nation," and "Our Nation's Dawning."

At school, we were given pencils, drinks, a treat, and tokens to commemorate the event celebrating our independence. We now had our motto: Together We Aspire, Together We Achieve. Our watchwords were *discipline*, *production*, and *tolerance*. Our governor-general was Sir Solomon Hochoy, and our prime minister was the

Right Honorable Dr. Eric Eustace Williams. Trinidad and Tobago's independence was celebrated with a great sense of national pride and joy.

On some holidays, I would go on what seemed to be an endlessly long journey by bus to visit my aunt who lived at Matelot, a village located on the northeastern coast of Trinidad, where I would pick coffee and cocoa, gather nutmeg, dig out the coconut from the shells and turn copra in a cocoa house, grate coconut to make oil, and go to the different parts of the estate on the backs of the donkeys my aunt's family owned. My mother ensured that her children attended church and Sunday school, made our First Communion, and were confirmed as "good Catholics." I would also vacation with my aunt and uncle at Santa Flora, a village in south Trinidad. There were ten members of their family. I loved when my uncle would sit in the gallery and strum his guitar, singing Negro spirituals like "Old Black Joe," "Swanee River," "Steal Away," and "Swing Low, Sweet Chariot." All the children would join in singing alto, soprano, bass, and tenor since they all sang at the Roman Catholic church choir.

As a child, I looked forward to the various holidays celebrated in Trinidad and Tobago. Christmas was a wonderful time, celebrating the birthday of Jesus Christ. From October Christmas songs such as "Jingle Bells," "White Christmas," and "Frosty the Snowman," along with "Joy to the World," "O Holy Night," "Away in a Manger," and many other Christmas carols and Christmas calypsos, would be heard on the radio, which mainly the rich owned. There was house-to-house caroling, where children dressed in red and white with red hoods and sometimes candles in their hands would go from house to house singing carols, thereby bringing Christmas tidings to those who would open their doors to welcome them. The stores were decorated with Christmas trees with cotton placed around the branches representing snow, although most people had never seen real snow, Trinidad being a tropical island where snow never fell. Christmas music would also be playing loudly in the stores. It was a festive time.

Most people cleaned their homes and decorated them with

new or special curtains and carpets, and sometimes new furniture bought especially for this season. There was hurried shopping for an assortment of gifts for both young and old. Then there is the cuisine that is always associated with this time of the year, for example, sorrel, ginger beer, ham, fruitcake, pastelle, paime, apples, and grapes. The ham was boiled and baked on Christmas Eve night, and the curtains were hung and cushions on chairs changed while singing or listening to *parang*. The blended scents of the new linoleum, plastic tablecloth, sorrel, ham, cake, and bread being baked were unique and unforgettable.

On Christmas morning, few missed the church service, after which came the eating and drinking, well-wishing, and revelry. Both Christians and non-Christians celebrated Christmas, with some promoting Santa Claus as the main attraction and others celebrating the birth of Jesus Christ. On Christmas Day, all hostilities and disputes between neighbors or families were forgotten. Homes were visited and gifts were exchanged amid wishes for a merry Christmas and a happy New Year. There was usually an atmosphere of love and goodwill.

Christmas was followed by Carnival, which is usually celebrated in the days before Ash Wednesday. This is the season when calypsos are sung in tents across Trinidad and Tobago and also heard frequently on the radio. When I was young, there would be competitions, queen shows, a kiddies' carnival, king and queen of bands, Mas Bands, Ole Mas, and traditional characters such as Pierrot Grenades, bookmen, Dame Lorraines, bats, and clowns. Jab-Jab, covered in mud or what looked like paint; Moko Jumbies; and minstrels were familiar sights on the two days of gay abandon and revelry. Vendors also got to ply their wares, whether ice cream, coconut drops, cassava pone, sugar cakes, or mauby drink and fruit juices which were among the delicacies that one could buy on the streets.

Point Fortin, San Fernando, Arima, Chaguanas, and other towns had their scaled-down versions. However, masqueraders from the surrounding districts from La Brea to Icacos all came to Point Fortin, which was a judging point for the various activities in the deep south. Without visiting these countries, one would get vivid insights into Rome, Greece, Africa, and other countries via the portrayals of the different bands: Ancient Rome, Somewhere in New Guinea, Zulu Warriors, Sioux Indians, Apache Warriors, War bands, Sailors Ashore, and SSS Marines led by Harold Saldenah, Stephen Lee Heung, George Bailey, and other bandleaders. At Point Fortin, we had our own Valentine Ferdinand, along with Androvas with his Devil Mas, Cowboy George with his band of singing minstrels, and others.

Another feature of Carnival is the steelpan, of which Trinidad and Tobago is considered the birthplace. Competitions are held during the buildup to Carnival, and the steelpan was frequently played at parties and on the streets on the actual two days of revelry. In Point Fortin, there were Tornadoes, Silver Stars, and Sun Valley, in whose pan yards there would be a nightly gathering of villagers listening to and supporting their favorite pan sides. I looked forward to and immensely enjoyed these outings.

At San Fernando, there were Fonclaire and Hatters, among others, while in the north one heard of Desperadoes, Renegades, Harmonites, and All-Stars, to name a few. The main attraction, however, was at Port of Spain, the capital city, where most of the visitors from the neighboring islands and tourists from various parts of the world were concentrated. Carnival in Trinidad and Tobago was often regarded as the greatest show on earth.

Another festival that was looked forward to was Divali, when homes were cleaned and clay pots with oil were lit in celebration of the Hindu goddess Lakshmi. For Divali, Indian sweets and delicacies are distributed among family, friends, and neighbors.

During cricket season, the men would be seen with their transistor radios listening to West Indies playing England or Australia and other teams around the world, coming out mostly victorious. I felt a sense of pride then, that a little island, often regarded as a dot in the ocean, could compete favorably with these much larger and more developed countries.

Life at this stage seemed to revolve around these festivals and activities. As a young adolescent, I was so caught up in them, and also with the people with whom I enjoyed them, my neighbors, relatives, and school friends, that this made up my whole world. I could not then conceive of living outside the repetitive rhythm of these events.

Country life was simple and humble, with great love and togetherness existing in our community. These early years, for me, were a time of innocence, naivete, and happiness. Racism and segregation were not largely practiced among the lower classes, nor was politics a major concern in our household. However, I feel that the seeds of rebellion were planted deep in my consciousness as I visualized the lives of the slaves and relived their pain. Little did I know that my world was about to be changed dramatically, in ways that I could never have imagined.

2

AWAKENING

Although I never had all my books for school, I was always at the top of my class. I always looked forward to All Saints' Day, when we would go to the cemetery to celebrate the dead. We would wait until families left and the candles on graves were out or partially burnt out, and then we'd collect them to use to provide light for studying since at home the kerosene lights or flambeaus that we used had to be put out by a certain time to save fuel out of economic necessity.

It was no surprise when in 1965 I passed the Common Entrance Examination to attend Point Fortin Intermediate Roman Catholic School, one of three successful students from my previous school that year. I was part of the school choir under Theresa Reyes and Ammon Joseph. We sang benediction hymns in Latin—"O Salutaris Hostea" and "Tantum ergo Sacramentum," among others—during the Thursday Mass. I was one of the children of Mary, and I recall Sister Paul Clarke, a nun, instilling strict moral values in us. She told us girls that our bodies were sacred and should only be given to our husbands. She also taught us that love is giving, not only of material things, but also of oneself: sharing, caring, and self-sacrificing, among other things. One had to attend Mass every Sunday since there was always the watchful eye of our form mistress Ms. Lystra Yuille, who never missed a service and seemed to be able to recall all those who did.

Ms. Yuille seemed to think I was a gifted child. I remember her taking me to the principal's office and introducing me, saying, "This child must possess native intelligence." Among my classmates were Western Rawlins, whose calypso sobriquet is "Cro Cro"; Penelope Robinson; and Esther Lucas. We were regarded as "government children," "a treacherous, dangerous, deceitful, bad bunch of rogues and vagabonds." She, our form mistress, meant well. This was strictly a Roman Catholic school, attended only by the elite of Point Fortin, that is, staunchly Roman Catholic children, Chinese children, and light-colored children from middle-class families. It was now opened up to the lower class and lower castes based on ability via the Common Entrance Examinations.

Choosing a career was not difficult since the options we had as females were limited to teaching, nursing, clerical and secretarial work, and other types of employment within the public service. The thought of attending university never crossed my mind, because apart from my family being financially challenged, the secondary school I attended did not possess a sixth form. I knew that I wanted to become a schoolteacher, which required me to pass four subjects, including English language. Therefore, I focused on obtaining five GCE passes despite the pleas of my form mistress that I should aim higher.

I was aware of the hippie movement of the 1960s and of the women's liberation groups that emerged from it. The music of the times, including "Say It Loud—I'm Black and I'm Proud" by James Brown; our local Lancelot Layne's "Blow Way," in which the lyrics go, "If a man wants to set false standards for you to follow, to he, what ya say? Blow way"; and calypsos, such as the Mighty Duke's "Black Is Beautiful" exhorted blacks to be proud of their skin color since as children, we were made to feel that being black was demeaning and degrading. The word *black* was applied to all that was bad, base, or ugly. If you were very dark, you were called "blackie corbeau," "tar baby," and "golliwog." White dolls with their pink skin, straight noses, and slim bodies were portrayed as the ideal. Blacks were most times ashamed of their skin color and their African features, wishing they were white.

The Mighty Sparrow's calypso "I Am a Slave," which captures

the cruel African slave experience in song, was among my favorites. I had heard of Martin Luther King Jr., Rosa Parks, Malcolm X, and some of the other black heroes of the American civil rights movement. They all had a tremendous influence on the early development of my consciousness and helped to shape my thinking.

It was amid this type of local and international environment when the status quo was being questioned and challenged and where nothing was being taken for granted any longer that I was growing up as a young adolescent. The music and lyrics of the songs of that period also exerted a tremendous influence on my thought process. I was now becoming more aware of the racism, injustices, and inequalities that existed around the world, including in my own country. Black people were now becoming more educated about their past and were now more vocal and willing to do whatever it took to right the wrongs in their societies. They were seeking to establish more equitable societies so that their children would not suffer as they did. The shame associated with their heritage was lessening, and they were becoming more accepting of themselves, which fact was communicated in the conscious, militant, and rebellious songs of the times.

Afro hairstyles and the wearing of dashikis and other African styles of dress were becoming the order of the day among many people of African descent. African drumming, black singers and musicians, and black poetry, as well as psychedelic lights and disco music, were popular among the youths. Listening to the Jackson Five, Aretha Franklin, Dionne Warwick, Diana Ross and the Supremes, and others evoked in me a great sense of pride for the black artists who seemed to be taking the music world by storm.

The Roman Catholic church at Point Fortin had as its parish priest Canon McNamara from Ireland. The church itself was a large and beautiful structure. As children, we boasted of Roman Catholics having the best church building. People at different levels of the social stratum attended. Seats to the front were reserved for the upper classes, while the lower classes were made to stand at the back despite the reserved seats being empty. I viewed this as discrimination against the poor.

Despite following all the rituals involved in the Mass, I did not understand what appeared to be very mysterious. I had my prayer book but felt that I needed to know more about the Bible, which was part of the reason that I studied religious knowledge as one of my chosen courses for the General Certificate Examination.

Just as changes were happening in the wider society, changes were also taking place in the church. The choir, of which I was a member, began singing folk songs, and altars were now turned around so that the priests were facing the congregation during the celebration of the Mass, which was now being said mostly in English instead of Latin.

In my community, I became involved in various youth groups: SPAY (Saint Patrick Assembly of Youths), the PNM (People's National Movement) youth group, and the Astral Sports and Cultural Club, to name a few. As a member of the Red Cross, I fainted when we had to line up along the streets of San Fernando and wave flags during Queen Elizabeth's visit to Trinidad in 1966.

I now began attending school bazaars, Dutch parties, and other house parties in addition to other social events such as weddings and christenings. I think I inherited my love for music and dancing from my father, who was an ardent musician.

I would attend political meetings, which were usually held when elections were upcoming. The first time I saw the prime minister in the flesh and heard him address a political meeting in my village, I was awed and filled with great admiration for the way he was able to speak for what seemed like hours without reading, and also the way he had memorized numbers. No wonder he was touted as "being the eighth brightest brain" in the world. I took an instant liking to him.

It was around this time that two brothers, Owen, and Rodney Monroe, came to live opposite my home. They specialized in handicrafts, making lovely coconut ashtrays and jewelry boxes, doing taxidermy, and working with crab and other shells. I would always go over and touch something I wasn't supposed to, always asking "What?" and "Why?"

To this, Rodney would often respond in colloquial vernacular:

"One of these days, you will stretch your gundi so far, you will end up in a Sunday callaloo."

Also around this time, I found myself questioning the values of society, the elders in my community, my friends' lifestyles, our sexuality, how sexuality found expression, heterosexual relationships, and double standards of the adults, all of whom seemed to be saying to young people, "Do as I say, not as I do."

I began asking myself, "Who am I?" I wanted to know why was I born into the family in which I was born and in the place where I was born. What was my purpose here? Was God real, and if so, where was he? Should I ask him to "stop the world and let me off" as per the lyrics to a popular song at the time? Many times, I would walk the beach alone or go into the nearby savannah and cry out to God. This quest led me to the writings of Norman Vincent Peale, for example, *On the Power of Positive Thinking*; Dale Carnegie, who wrote and lectured on self-improvement, interpersonal skills, and public speaking; and Kahlil Gibran, for example, *The Prophet*, and the works of T. Lobsang Rampa the Zen Buddhist, for answers.

Previously, my reading literature consisted of Grimm fairy tales, romance novels published by Mills & Boon and/or written by Barbara Cartland, espionage novels written by Mickey Spillane, and spy fiction featuring Modesty Blaise, among others. I was trying to find meaning in my life and my place in this cosmos.

My class teacher had migrated to Canada, leaving a void deep within me as he was one of my male role models. Initially, some of us kept corresponding with him. After some time, the letters became fewer and arrived farther apart.

The Black Power uprising of 1970 occurred during the time I was preparing for my GCE O-level exams. I attended a meeting where there was talk about the haves and have-nots, the control of the commanding heights of the economy by foreigners, and the externally propelled nature of the economy of Trinidad and Tobago. They also spoke of foreign interest in the town of Point Fortin, the starving wages being paid to workers, and the exploitation to which the working class was subjected. Tubal Uriah Buzz Butler, a past leader of the trade union movement, and his struggle for bread in the oil belt were also referred to. I had met a few friends and we "limed" or chatted for most of the meeting.

The following Thursday, I was on my way to school when I encountered a march being led by Michael Als, leader of the Young Power Movement. He was one of the main speakers at the meeting which I had attended the week before. He had a microphone through which he urged the crowd to be disciplined, telling them that others would join them along the way. Red, black, yellow, and green flags were being carried by the marchers who wore dashikis and other forms of African wear and had their hair in Afro and Indo hairstyles. Placards bearing phrases such as "Valdez Must Go," "Down with Capitalism," "End Foreign Exploitation," "Africans and Indians, Unite," "Power to the People," and "Nationalize Now" were prominent. Their destination was Port of Spain.

It was amid these marches and meetings that I wrote my exams. Since my family and I did not buy daily newspapers, I was only vaguely aware of most of the activities being engaged in. There was graffiti on the walls and placards bearing the rhetoric "Power to the people," "Power comes out of the barrel of a gun," and "Armed revolution is the only solution," which were being spouted at the time. Buildings were being burnt, looting was engaged in, and people were being arrested and detained, all of which I tried to keep abreast of but my exams were my main focus. There was also the fact that most of the activities were concentrated in the north while I lived in the south of Trinidad.

On my way to school, I sometimes passed in front of a bookshop on Agard Road. This shop was frequented by dashiki-clad young men and women wearing Afro and Indo hairstyles like those who had previously engaged in the march. It had always aroused my curiosity.

Negroes were now beginning more and more to accept themselves, and mothers, daughters, and sisters began wearing African prints and "Jesus sandals," the soles of which were made from car tires. Their hairstyles were natural instead of pressed out with a hot iron. African brothers and sisters were changing their English names to

African names with meaning. They were also giving their children African names. The wearing of lipstick and of rouge on the cheeks and the use of bleaching cream to become fairer were fast becoming things of the past among conscious African sisters. This period was characterized by the music of popular black singers: "Hard Road to Travel" by Jimmy Cliff, a Jamaican reggae singer, "Hello, Africa" by Eddie Grant of Guyana, and "We the People Who Are Darker than Blue" by Curtis Mayfield of the United States, among others. These songs served to escalate my identification with my African roots and with the whole Black Consciousness Movement.

On December 1, 1970, my eighteenth birthday, I began teaching at a primary school at Fanny Village, Point Fortin. I was very involved with children since my elder sister used to run a preschool. I had taken a liking to children and felt that helping to mold young minds was a special privilege. The children and I would often go on educational rambles, that is, treks to the nearby beach, where we would explore shells, sea cockroaches, and caves that lined the shore, and investigate other forms of marine life. Hiking to the hills and observing nature in the form of birds' nests, leaves, ants, insects, plants, and birds was another of the adventures we engaged in. Other classes eagerly joined us.

A house system was established in which children were grouped into houses and adjudged for being well-groomed with clean and neat school attire and with clean fingernails that were cut short. A portion of the schoolyard was also assigned to them, for which they had the responsibility of ensuring it remained litter-free. House tests were conducted in various subjects for which points were given. The house to which Desi, my male counterpart, and I were assigned always won the most points.

As a teacher, I tried to instill in my students the importance of neatness and tidiness. I also always emphasized commitment to schoolwork. Once during a visit by the inspector of schools, she called all the other teachers in upon seeing the books of my students and told them that that was how books were to be kept. She then asked my class if they knew of any recitations. All hands went up.

They did "Someone" by Walter de la Mare. She then asked for another, which was answered by a student's recitation of "There Was an Indian." Another request was subsequently made for a song, and all hands were raised. A very brave student named Lloydie sang "John Boulay" while the class sang the chorus. This was followed by "Zinda Geet," an East Indian song, sung by another student called Harry. The superintendent was so impressed that she made me choir mistress for infants and for the junior and senior classes.

I loved children dearly. I encouraged them to ask questions. I would place a box on my desk in which they would put their questions, then I would reserve time at the end of the day for answers, which were mainly provided by the class with guidance from me. The school had a problem with burglary; therefore, I kept all books, chalk, dusters, etc., for my classroom at home. The neighbors were amazed at the crowds of children who frequented my home before and after school, competing to be allowed the privilege of carrying the items.

On Saturdays, I gave Common Entrance Examination lessons free of charge to underprivileged children who were preparing to write the entrance exams, which would enable them to enter the secondary school system without having to pay for that aspect of their education. I would also assist with postprimary classes whenever a teacher was absent. Mr. Calpu, the principal at the time, was gentle and nurturing, giving people space to grow. This was evidenced by the opportunities presented to me to become choir mistress and sports mistress, presiding over sports, including netball, football, cricket, table tennis, and track and field.

One morning, I was told that there was someone in the front yard of the school building asking for me. On arriving at the front yard, I was confronted by a buxom woman whom I had never before set eyes upon. She seemed to be middle-aged, was neatly dressed, and had her head wrapped with a brightly colored headscarf. As I entered the courtyard, she began walking toward me. With a very serious expression on her face, she inquired in a very hostile tone, "Are you Miss Jacob?"

I responded, "Yes, I am," while trying to do a quick assessment of the person and the situation. Her next words left me flabbergasted.

"Woman, what have you done to my child?"

I was taken aback.

"What is the name of your child?" I hesitantly responded. On seeing the bewildered look on my face, she burst out laughing. She then went on to introduce herself and explain that she was the mother of the little girl who usually had lunch at my home, my former student. I had taught her daughter in the infant department during my first year at the school. She never moved away from me. She would come to my home at lunchtime and would tell me how much she liked my food. Eventually, I stopped her from bringing her lunch from home.

I learned that morning that at home, this girl spoke incessantly of her teacher and would refuse her snacks if she did not get one for "my miss," as she referred to me. Her mother stated that she had to see in the flesh this person who was so loved by and had had such a tremendous influence on her daughter. Other students had also become very attached to me because I took the time to listen to their stories, instill values, provide guidance, and sincerely care for them.

In heterosexual relationships, I could not find the qualities I was seeking in a man. All of them seemed to be sexually motivated. The advice given to me by the Catholic nun had stayed with me for a long time, despite the fact that most of my friends with whom I went to school were sexually active, some already having children.

By this time, my mother, who had been very strict with my other siblings, had relaxed a bit. The others always accused her of letting me get away with things that they did not dare do while growing up. One time my eldest sister, who was already engaged to be married, went to a Carnival celebration with her in-laws and her fiancé could not get a taxi to return her home (there were no telephones, cell phones, or other modern technology at that time). When she returned home the next morning, she was called every name there was to describe a loose woman or *jal*, despite her tears and her pleas that she had not slept in the same room with her fiancé.

Left: Andrea Jacob after finishing secondary school in 1970.

3

1970 REVOLUTION

It was while I was visiting my friend Rodney toward the end of 1970 that I heard him speak of one of his friends who was a political detainee in prison whom he intended to visit. He went on to show me a letter written to him by this friend, whose name was Michael Als. The letter was written on prison stationery, and its contents were filled with love. In the letter, Michael addresses Rodney as "brother" and refers to their "brothers" both inside and outside of prison, encouraging Rodney to keep the faith. "The struggle," revolution, and "the masses" are also mentioned.

I was greatly inspired by this letter, which communicated so much love, sincerity, and selflessness that it highly aroused my curiosity, causing a spark to be lit. It turned out that Michael was the leader of the Young Power Movement in Trinidad and was the same person I had heard addressing the marchers previously. He was a schoolteacher and owner of a bookstore and handicraft shop where my friend Rodney sold his crafts, the same place where I used to see the young men and women garbed in African attire assembling. The bookstore was the meeting place for the Young Power Movement.

Michael was released from prison shortly after that, and I was invited to a meeting by my friend Rodney, which I attended. Michael, who was also at the meeting, was tall, handsome, brown-skinned, and bespectacled. He was dressed in a dashiki and wore his hair in a large Afro hairstyle. He had a lisp and was a very charismatic speaker. It was obvious that the other members of the movement idolized him. The group discussed the direction the movement should take following the events of 1970. In addition to the craft shop, electrical repair shop, and bookstore that they managed, they proposed to expand by including a provision shop. The land and an old house were obtained for its construction.

During this meeting, everyone was referred to as either brother or sister, and I had the opportunity to meet face-to-face some of those dashiki-clad, Afro-coiffed people I had previously only seen in passing. The bookshop contained an assortment of literature on black history and revolution. I remember paying special attention to books such as the Kaywana series by Edgar Mittleholzer; Frantz Fanon's *Wretched of the Earth* and *Black Skin, White Masks*; Angela Davis's *If They Come in the Morning*; Malcolm X's *Black Revolt*; and Eldridge Cleaver's *Soul on Ice*. This provided the foundation for my involvement in the Young Power Movement. My social and political consciousness was truly in the process of awakening.

This group, at the front of the Young Power Movement, subsequently merged with the National Organization of Revolutionary Students and changed its name to Youth Forces and Working-Class Movement. It was at one of these meetings that I met with one Arthur Napoleon Robinson, who was later to become prime minister, and then president, of the Republic of Trinidad and Tobago.

I was given the task of collecting newspaper clippings from the daily newspapers and compiling a scrapbook of the events leading up to the revolution, those during, and those after. This I engaged in enthusiastically since it allowed me to catch up on the readings that I had missed while the events were unfolding in real time. I was able to get more in-depth knowledge of the Black Power revolution of Trinidad and Tobago and the protest marches in Port of Spain that began in support of the Trinidadian students who were engaged in a struggle against racism and discrimination in Canada.

These students had protested by locking themselves in the computer room and were subsequently charged with setting fire to the computer center at Sir George Williams University in Montreal, Canada. I had a special interest in this occurrence because this was the university where my past form teacher had been a student at the time the events took place. In addition, one of the accused was a relative of mine. In the process of compiling the scrapbook, I read of Geddes Granger, whose name was changed to Makandal Daaga, leader of the National Joint Action Committee (NJAC) and the Black Power movement of 1970.

The invasion of the Cathedral of the Immaculate Conception on Independence Square was of great significance since the cathedral was regarded as the biggest symbol of the white power structure. This action resulted in the arrests of eight demonstrators, who were charged with both disturbing a place of worship and incitement.

There were National Joint Action Committee meetings at Woodford Square, which were followed by marches to shantytown, accompanied by shouts of "Power to the people!" with upraised clenched right fists punching the air. This had snowballed into marches consisting of tens of thousands of young and not so young brothers and sisters who were being unofficially educated in the "University of Woodford Square," which was a park in the heart of Port of Spain, the capital city, often used as a meeting place for the grassroots protestors who would engage in ideology sharing and sometimes have heated discussions about social ills and the other issues that were being highlighted and vented there. There was the calling in of police and the Riot Squad to control the large attendant crowds.

Molotov cocktails were thrown at the homes of the then education minister and the US vice-consul, and other homes. Marches to San Juan, Laventille Hill, and Belmont followed, the longest of which was one to Caroni, with the main objective being the unity of Africans and Indians.

There was also a march led by Michael Als to the Prime Minister's Office at Whitehall and then to Balisier House. Other marches included those to Petit Valley, Carenage, Saint Clair, and Federation and Ellerslie Parks. Then there was the return of some of the students from Sir George Williams University and the victory rally that followed. Eric Williams's first speech on the Black Power movement indicated that while people had the right to march, they did not have the right to trample on other people's freedoms.

I read of the open confrontation between the police and the Black Power demonstrators and of the demands by the NJAC for food, shelter, employment, dignity, a place in the political structure, a right to be part of the economy, and room for the black man.

There were more marches, from Port of Spain to Arima and from Scarborough to Charlottesville, which involved the smashing of store windows in Scarborough and the throwing of Molotov cocktails at the home of the then president of the Tobago Chamber of Commerce.

There was the shooting of Basil Davis, a young militant Black Power supporter, in a "confrontation with police." There was also the arrest of seventeen in San Fernando after Black Power demonstrations erupted in violence. The subsequent funeral of Basil Davis was attended by thousands.

A concert was staged by Mahalia Jackson, a popular black American gospel singer, in Queen's Park, Savannah, and there was the resignation of A. N. R. Robinson, then minister of external affairs, from the cabinet. On April 21, 1970, there was a declaration by the government of a state of emergency as well as a dusk-to-dawn curfew. Twenty-four Black Power leaders had been arrested and were subsequently taken to Nelson Island. This resulted in a downtown window-smashing spree.

Additionally, there was the mutiny at Tetron, the Trinidad and Tobago Regiment Headquarters, led by Lieutenants Rafique Shah and Rex La Salle. There was the leading of a convoy of army vehicles by rebel soldiers heading for Port of Spain, then the shelling of the hillside above the convoy by the *Trinity*, a coast guard fast patrol boat, to try to block its passage. This was met with machine-gun fire, resulting in the decapitation of a private by shrapnel after a shell exploded into a cluster of nearby trees. Following this, the rebels returned to Tetron. During all these happenings, Venezuelan military vessels were sighted approaching Trinidad, while the USS *Guadalcanal* was asked to retreat after entering Trinidadian waters.

During this time, with the availability of books at the bookshop, I read most of Edgar Mittelholzer's Kaywana series, which tells of plantation structure and the life of the slaves, including revolts, riots, and beatings. I read all about the Cuban Revolution led by Fidel Castro, the overthrow of Fulgencio Batista, and the guerrilla war fought in the Sierra Maestra. I also read of Che Guevara and his part as a guerrilla leader and trainer, and of the Black Jacobins and Toussaint Louverture of Haiti. Additionally, there were books on the civil rights movement in the United States. I read works by Martin Luther King Jr. expressing his dream for the United States, in which he foresaw little black children and little white children walking the streets of their nation together as friends.

I also read of the Black Panther movement, and Stokely Carmichael, a Trinidadian, who was banned from entering the country because of his involvement in this movement. My other readings included Rosa Parks and her struggle against racism—her not giving up her seat on the bus because she was black, and the subsequent bus strike. I read Angela Davis, the Soledad Brothers, and Malcolm X, and of the Mangrove Nine trial in England, where a group of nine British black activists were tried for inciting a riot during a 1970 protest against the police's targeting of the Mangrove, a Caribbean restaurant in Notting Hill, West London. The defendants included two Trinidadians, Althea Jones-Lecointe and Darcus Howe. There was apartheid in South Africa and the imprisonment of Nelson Mandela; the struggles of Winnie, his wife, in Soweto; and the struggles of other African nations such as Angola, Zimbabwe, and Tanzania, which were all engaged in a liberation struggle to free their people from foreign domination and exploitation. The war in Vietnam was a major event at this time too.

Closer to home, there were the struggles of our neighbors in the Caribbean who had a similar history of slavery and revolt. Walter Rodney of Guyana and his signature book *How Europe Underdeveloped Africa* gave me a clear understanding of and insight into multinational corporations and capitalism. These works I've mentioned were all part of my literary diet, and they left me with an insatiable craving for more.

I was now being increasingly educated about what I considered to be the real world, getting a better understanding of the system of exploitation within which I was growing up. In addition, the inequalities in society were being exposed and better understood. My worldview was changing rapidly.

This was the global reality amid which I was growing up. I had to find my part in it all. So now it became not just reading, but also sharing the knowledge I gained with others. The authors I was reading were all people who had a history of slavery and colonialism, racism, oppression, and exploitation and who had experienced all the social ills that are part and parcel of the capitalist system. The people were now becoming more aware or conscious via education. They wanted to play their part in charting their own destiny and attempt to break the shackles that had them living defeated lives. They wanted their freedom by any means necessary.

This was the wind of change that was blowing. The music, the songs, and the language all spoke of it. In her song, Roberta Flack called it the "trade winds," while Jimmy Cliff sang of the "synthetic world we're living in."

I also read of the Roman Catholic priests of South America who had left the priesthood to join the freedom fighters, one of whom was Camillo Torres. I remember when our own Roman Catholic archbishop, Anthony Pantin, wanted to join the marches during the Black Power demonstration but decided against doing so at the last minute. There were also writings by the Brazilian educator Paulo Freire, for example, *Pedagogy of the Oppressed*, and works by other writers on liberation theology or radical Christianity.

Back then, I saw Jesus Christ as the greatest revolutionary since he did not conform to the social order of the day. His concern for the poor and the oppressed and the communal living of the early church, to my mind, paralleled communism. However, I had issues with the use of firearms as a means of bringing about liberation and freedom.

Having been familiar with the Holy Bible, I found the thought of Peter cutting off the ear of one of Jesus's persecutors on his way to Calvary, and Jesus's reaction to this, which was to reattach the ear, lingering with me. Jesus's saying that "those who live by the sword shall die by the sword" was another scripture that created conflict in my mind given my religious upbringing. Karl Marx's thoughts about religion being the opiate of the people, that is, something to keep them in a state of passivity so that they could be easily exploited by the capitalist system, had me thinking that if this present system were no more, then true Christianity could be practiced.

I also searched the Bhagavad Gita for meaning, reading about the age of Kali, with the Bhagavad Gita putting forward the view that when unrighteousness prevails, warriors rise to fight against it as depicted in the battle between Arjuna and Krishna. Another holy book spoke of killing the aggressor who was coming to you. Despite trying to appease my mind, however, I found there was conflict, and I had no desire to displease God. I only wanted to fulfill my cosmic purpose.

4

INTRODUCTION TO "THE ORGANIZATION"

Toward the latter part of 1970, I met John Bedeau while attending a social event. Although there was music and dancing, he just stood in a corner as though surveying the place. He eventually came over, said "good evening," and asked me to dance. I learned that night that he had obtained eight O-level passes and had taken four subjects at A-level from Saint Mary's College, one of the country's most prestigious schools. At that time, he was employed at the University of the West Indies–Saint Augustine.

Our conversation had gravitated to the topic of transportation, which led me to say, "I love motorbikes! I want to purchase one."

He scoffed. "I have seen too many motorbike casualties at the general hospital where I worked. A car would be a much safer option." I didn't reply, but I considered what he had to say. He also informed me that he had relatives in the south with whom he had just begun to reestablish relationships and had intentions of visiting shortly. It turned out that they were school friends of mine. He and I chatted and danced for the rest of the time. I looked forward to seeing him again. I gave him my permission to visit my home on his next trip to the south. Among the information we shared was the fact that he was born on the last day of the first month, while I was born on the first day of the last month. We concluded that this was no coincidence: we were predestined to meet. This was the beginning of a relationship that would go on to play a major part in the life-changing events that followed.

The next Saturday morning, a few days after my return home, to my pleasant surprise, in response to being told that I had a visitor, I went to the front door to find "Johnny," as he was called by his close acquaintances. He was standing in the yard wearing a sleeveless red jersey. His hair, instead of the previous Afro hairstyle, was now plaited in thick braids, and he was wearing a pair of blue jeans that were cut off at the knees and were held at the waist with a thick red cord. On his feet, he wore push-toe or Jesus sandals with thick rubber soles, and a silver bracelet on his left wrist. One could not have asked for a more unconventional, radical look.

At that time, I lived with my mother and eight-year-old sister. Our home then was a three-bedroom wooden house built by my mother after years of sacrifice. I remember when we moved in after living in several rented rooms. There was only one room enclosed by sheets of galvanized steel and board with a ladder for steps. It was now finally complete. How my mother had managed to do it on a thirty-dollar-per-month salary with seven children to support is still miraculous to me. I was unsure of how my mother would react to my visitor, who was so unconventionally dressed; hence, I decided to get him away as soon as possible. I suggested to Johnny that he and I go for a walk along the beach, which was about four hundred meters from where I lived, which we did.

From the moment I laid my eyes on him, I knew that Johnny was different. He had an air of mystery about him, which intrigued me. His response to some of my questions was that he could not answer, or he'd simply smile. This only served to stoke my curiosity. We talked about Mills & Boon, the books I had read in the past and recently, and the fact that life did not usually have a happily-ever-after ending. He said that I must not believe everything that is written in a book but that I should question everything: Why was it written? By whom? Whose interest or purposes does it serve? What is the writer's agenda?

After a lengthy discussion on the present socioeconomic

situation, Johnny and I analyzed and discussed what we considered to be errors of the 1970 revolution, the fact that after the leaders were arrested, the masses had no direction and identified a need to develop the leadership potential of each individual so that they could use their own initiative to act should a future situation arise where such a thing would become necessary. We agreed that African descendants needed to understand their history and, in so doing, find their identities and be proud of their heritage. People should know their past to understand their present situation and be able to plan for the future. However, Johnny said, the major problem faced by Trinidad and Tobago was not one of race, but one of class, namely, the class system that resulted from our history of slavery and colonialism and the capitalists' mode of production. It had to do with the relationship between the owners of the means of production and the working class, the haves vs. the have-nots.

We also discussed the state's response to the then recent uprisings, in addition to the beatings, arrests, and frame-ups and people's inability to assemble. We talked about the events of the Black Power movement, how it made an impact on the population, our involvement, and the direction we felt that the struggle should now take. I told Johnny about my involvement with the Youth Forces and Working-Class Movement. He spoke of a large number of very militant young people out there who were getting frustrated and channeling their frustration into drug abuse and "rope" or violence after undergoing consciousness awakening via the events leading to the 1970 revolution. They were now without direction but were very conscious and militant.

There also existed many political organizations at the time, among which were the New Beginning Movement, the Coordinating Council, Embryo, the URO (Union of Revolutionary Organizations), UMROBI (United Movement for the Reconstruction of Black Identity), TAPIA (Tapia House), YFWCM (Youth Forces and Working-Class Movement), and NJAC (National Joint Action Committee).

A considerable amount of educating of the people was being done by these revolutionary groups via publications and their newspapers. A lot of "block" gatherings on street corners and discussions were held, although some revolutionary literature they were circulating was regarded as subversive. Johnny expressed the view that any organization had to work underground as a consequence of the level of violence that was being unleashed by the police on people who were suspected of plotting, organizing, or supporting the revolution.

These people, he said, were now being organized into cells or units throughout the country clandestinely since people were not allowed to gather to hold meetings following the recent unrest. We both felt that we had a lot in common in terms of our ideologies and our wanting to be a part of the solution instead of contributing to the problem by inaction. That provided the basis for our relationship.

Johnny seemed to possess limitless knowledge, and while he and I were working together, I felt there was much that I needed to know. Johnny emphasized that one should read to look at what others had done to achieve their liberation, such as Fidel Castro in Cuba and the Tupamaros in Latin America, Mozambique, Tanzania, and all the Third World countries that were struggling against capitalism and imperialism, and try to work out an ideology suitable to Trinidad and Tobago with its many contradictions of race, ethnicity, class, religion, culture, etc. We were not to seek to impose any ideology lock, stock, and barrel on Trinidad and Tobago.

Johnny spoke of his involvement with a "Krall" at Bushe Street San Juan, where he lived, a place where economic activities were conducted via a fruit and vegetable stall and that functioned as a meeting place for the "brothers and sisters" to discuss and educate each other on political and other activities. He mentioned "prowls" in the Northern Range but would not elaborate. I visited him one day up north and was taken to a house where I was introduced as "a sister from the south." After questioning glances were exchanged among the three occupants of the room, I was left in the living room while they went into another room.

Talk about guns, transport, the other brothers (or "mankind), etc., followed. It all seemed coded. I did not mind that I was not included as I felt that this was necessary security. I was subsequently taken to another block at San Juan, where I met a few more brothers. They appeared cool and relaxed. During Johnny's absence from the room, I seized the opportunity to ask whether they belonged to the same organization. The awkwardness that followed caused me to regret having asked the question the minute it left my lips. They changed the topic after politely suggesting that I ask Johnny. This way, they cleverly evaded my questions.

Later that night I realized that Johnny had been informed that I'd asked questions. He told me that in the future I should direct my questions to him. I could see that he was upset. I felt embarrassed and resolved not to let this reoccur. From then on I spoke even less and used my senses more.

Despite all these things, I was getting a better understanding of struggles in the different parts of the world and their impact on the Caribbean, on Trinidad and Tobago, and particularly on me as a young person growing up in this society amid it all. A great deal was now being put into perspective, and therefore I better understood it. I began gravitating more and more away from the Youth Forces and Working-Class Movement and toward "the organization." I was eager and excited about these new developments.

One day I accompanied a brother to Sea Lots, or shantytown as it was called. This resulted in what one could call culture shock on my part. I had not been all that familiar with Port of Spain and its environs. I had heard of ghettos, but nothing could have prepared me for what I saw that day. I had thought that growing up in the country and not having some of the finer things in life was being poor, but this opened my eyes to what real poverty was. The houses were made of wood, galvanized steel sheeting, boxes, and apparently whatever the residents were able to get their hands on. The dwellings were in such proximity to each other, and so dilapidated, that privacy was nonexistent in most cases. The children were mostly dirty and in various stages of nakedness. They went barefoot and played with makeshift toys of different sorts. However, the adults were warm and welcoming, and like the children, they were filled with love and were willing to share what little they had.

I could not believe that this was happening in Trinidad and that people lived under these conditions. We spent the greater part of the day at that place. I left with such a deep feeling of love and togetherness that has stayed with me up to today. In the days, weeks, and months that followed, I would cry when thinking of the living conditions of these people while listening to the songs "Patches" and "In the Ghetto." We made other visits to Laventille and other impoverished parts of Trinidad, but that experience had a tremendous effect on the way I viewed people and life. It deepened my resolve and commitment to be a part of the struggle to help alleviate poverty in the world.

Since the organization was growing with units scattered throughout the country, some of the brothers suggested that we form a unit with the unaligned brothers in my area since I had already been holding discussions with them about ideology and shared literature with them. It was felt that this new unit need not be large since a chain is as strong as its weakest link and one or two sound members could be more effective than twenty with one weak one.

Very soon we had a unit with about ten inner circle members. I was the only female. A semiurban guerilla unit, we began conducting political and first aid classes on an almost daily basis. Johnny and other brothers from the north would come to assist and provide guidance. Because of rising inflation and associated price increases, we embarked on projects to make goods and services available to the masses at lower costs.

We shared the view that by working and living together as a unit, we would be able to strip ourselves and each other of what we referred to as "Second World values," the aim being to develop a model of the new person whose values would be based on brotherly love instead of selfishness and greed. Abuse of wives, girlfriends, sisters, or children was prohibited among us. The men were also encouraged to assume their roles as providers and protectors, while the "village ram" mentality was frowned upon. Sisters were expected to respect themselves and others. Lying and stealing were not engaged in, while sharing with and caring for each other became natural occurrences. These were among the unwritten rules by which we lived.

We began an agricultural project, pooled our resources, and emphasized communal living. There were plans afoot to obtain a fishing boat. I felt that this was similar to the communal living among the early Christians mentioned in the Bible. Throughout I continued to seek parallels between revolution and Christianity. I felt that we revolutionaries were the "salt of the earth" mentioned in the Bible.

On many sleepless nights, I thought of my father, who had died when I was still a child. I had heard stories of him working on the building of the Panama Canal and of workers returning home with miniature Union Jack flags in their pockets, which made them popular among the women. I heard of him sleeping in trees to avoid tigers in the Maracaibo Forest. I remember hearing of his involvement in the labor riots, his sleeping under "Dead Man's Bridge" awaiting those who broke the strike lines, and the beatings the scabs were given. I felt proud to be part of that militant stock. I thought of those who survived the Middle Passage, their fighting spirit and determination to overcome, and the system that continues to produce slaves and continues to exploit the labor power of the masses to appease the selfish greed of a few. Weren't all men brothers and created equal?

We began studying the writings of Mao Tse-tung, chairman of the Communist Party of China. Chairman Mao was a revolutionary who became the founding father of the People's Republic of China. His books include *On Guerrilla Warfare*, *Mao on Practice and Contradictions*, and *Quotations from Chairman Mao*. We also studied books by Joseph Stalin, the general secretary of the Communist Party of the Soviet Union; Vladimir Lenin, a Russian communist revolutionary; Georg Hegel, a German idealist; Karl Marx and Frederick Engels, writers of *The Communist Manifesto* and *Das Kapital*; and Yevgeni Preobrazhensky's *The ABC of Communism*.

Marxian class theory, which asserts that an individual's position within a class hierarchy is determined by his or her role in the production process and argues that political and ideological consciousness is determined by class position, was also studied with Trinidad and Tobago in mind. Books on guerrilla warfare became a staple. Carlos Marighella's *Guerrilla Warfare*, Robert Tabor's *The War of the Flea*, and Che Guevara's *Guerrilla Warfare* were also among the popular literature we examined.

We looked at slavery more deeply, including its implications and ramifications, its psychological effects on the people, and how these could be turned around or undone.

5

COMMITMENT

On the weekends when Johnny did not come to the south, he ensured that another brother from a unit in the east came down. This latter brother was well-liked by the other brothers and spent the weekend on many occasions. When I realized that Johnny carried a gun, I tried not to appear surprised and casually inquired about its origin. He mentioned that it had been "liberated" from the security department at the bus company, with a brief smile.

Not long after, while sitting on the block, he was "rubbed down" or searched by the police, who found the gun in his waistband. He was subsequently charged with robbery and possession of the weapon. There was to be a meeting to determine the next steps. Following the meeting, Johnny explained that there was a lot of organizational work to be done outside of prison and he felt that he would be more effective on the outside. Therefore, it was suggested by "mankind" and the other brothers, some for whom the police were searching, that he should jump bail and join those other brothers in the hills.

Since guerrilla warfare is an extension of politics by way of armed conflict and is a major weapon to achieve revolution, that is, to forcibly overthrow the government in order to introduce a new system, there was the need to educate and mobilize the people. On the other hand, there was the vanguard arm of NUFF (the National United Freedom Fighters), those who had been prematurely forced into that position by the violence meted out to them and others, a unit that urgently need to be consolidated. I was still unaware of the full extent of the organization or the magnitude of the support systems in place. Therefore, I felt that it was Johnny's decision to make. He chose not to attend court.

Subsequently, he underwent a name change and told me that he was given the name "N." I was curious as to the meaning behind this name and the reason for its choice. He tried to convince me that it was short for Nigel, but his sheepish look and body language betrayed him. I kept probing, until he eventually explained that as in mathematics, mankind felt that he had infinite knowledge, that is, knowledge to the nth power. His modesty made it difficult for him to explain, but to me, it was most appropriate. He was now referred to as "N."

Over time I learned that there were militant brothers wanted by the police for political activities during and after the 1970 revolution, who sought refuge in the Northern Range and also in Fyzabad in south Trinidad. The arms cache found in Lady Chancellor Hill and the guerillas in Fyzabad all concerned "the organization"; they were part of its military arm or vanguard. They had to be supplied with transportation, safe places to stay, and foodstuffs. Sometimes they would come down from the hills or "heights" to the "flats" or the community, at which time police who had gotten word of their whereabouts would attack them in what the police considered a "shootout." Other organization members or at times just friends in their company would flee with them to escape police brutality, thereby also becoming "wanted." Others would join them to avoid police harassment after becoming "hot," which meant that they were being investigated by the police.

Johnny emphasized that the police were also our brothers, but they were on the other side of the fence. We had relatives, friends, and neighbors among them. The real enemy was not the police but the system that we were up against. The objective, however, was not confrontation with the police at this point, but to build the organization from its roots while laying the foundation for a new social order.

One Saturday while out with friends, I received word that there had been a shootout with the police where men were killed and others were wounded. Johnny was involved. I immediately returned home, called for a meeting, and informed the unit. Since there were no cell phones at the time, this information had to be relayed via word of mouth to the others in a clandestine manner. I subsequently accompanied Johnny's aunt "Lell," who was a Seventh-day Adventist but would help the organization in any way she could, to a house at Long Circular, the house where I had met Johnny for the first time. Once there, I spoke with the neighbors and checked the house. There were bandages and medication among the items left behind. All the leatherette chairs had been slashed in the police's search.

The house had been turned upside down. Conversations with the neighbors revealed that unbeknownst to them at the time, there were wanted men staying at the house. They had only discovered this when police and the army surrounded the house early that morning and began calling the occupants out by name, telling them that they knew that they were in there and asking them to come out with their hands in the air. The only one to obey those orders was the owner of the house. He was shot, while the others escaped. I returned home and waited. It was a most agonizing few days.

Within the following week, a white Nissan 120Y with four occupants came to my home. It was driven by Clyde Haynes, who was now a regular visitor to our unit. There was also the brother from the Tunapuna unit known as Chipo, a brother called Ulric Gransaul, and a tall, slim, fair-skinned, elegantly dressed bespectacled sister whose name was Ruth Bayley. I had heard about this sister, who had links with the Coordinating Council and had been with the group from its inception. She wore her hair in a large Afro hairstyle and could have been considered an Angela Davis look-alike. These three individuals brought greetings from Johnny. They encouraged us to keep strong, and they gave me three books: *Guerrilla Warfare* by Carlos Marighella, *The American Revolt* by Malcolm X, and Robert Tabor's *War of the Flea*.

About two days later, a brother from a block in the east came to inform me that Johnny had sent for me. This time I made sure that I did not ask too many questions. We journeyed to Port of Spain to a one-room downstairs apartment at Village Council Street, Laventille. Johnny opened the door. Words cannot express the feelings that engulfed me. He looked very vulnerable. His plaits were gone; he wore a low haircut, had lost considerable weight, and looked very pale. I was speechless. After Johnny, my companion, and I exchanged greetings and chatted for a short while, my escort left, promising to return.

There was a mattress on the floor, and the room had one entrance—the front door. There was no other exit. I compared the shooting range of the self-loading rifles and submachine guns, which the police carried, and of the .45 revolver in Johnny's possession. This caused me to comment that this was suicide. He responded that there weren't many options. He informed me that there had been a shootout at Blanchisseuse involving the brothers and the police, in which police intercepted a maxi taxi being used to transport mankind. One brother, Hillary Valentine, perished. Johnny was shot through one side of his chest, and the bullet exited through the other side and lodged itself in another brother.

Following this incident, the brothers went to Dibe Long Circular, where they received medical attention. After about a week there, word got out: someone told someone, and the police were informed. A joint police and army team confronted the brothers at about three o'clock in the morning. Five of the occupants escaped unharmed through the back, where the army was concentrated. However, the owner of the house who went out with his hands in the air toward the front, where the police were concentrated, was shot in the shoulder at point-blank range.

After this encounter, there was another shooting, this one at Lopinot. This time Johnny was again shot, and the bullet lodged itself under his eye. The house had been surrounded. After being hit, he ran out into the bushes at the back of the house. He was wearing a pair of brown sneakers with white tips. While lying on his back, he could see the tips of his shoes standing out in the moonlight. He heard the police dogs approaching, barking. When they came upon him, he said to himself, "This is it," and closed his eyes, awaiting what seemed to be the inevitable. In the split second that followed, he said, he saw his whole life flash before his eyes. Silence followed, and the dogs began retreating, having been called off. Johnny was able to make his escape. Another brother, Joel de Masiah, was killed by the police during this encounter.

During the days that followed, I kept listening to the song "(If Loving You Is Wrong) I Don't Want to Be Right," but inserting my own words. These were young men putting their lives on the line for a better society, many with O-level and A-level passes. They were not ordinary criminals but were people with a vision for a better society and a better world, and they were playing their part in bringing it about. I also felt that I had a part. If loving my country and my brothers was wrong, I didn't want to be right. There was a purpose for my life. Was this the part I was to play?

I gave serious thought to my family. My mother had slaved in white people's kitchens to send me to school. I was the only one in the immediate family with a secondary school education; I was the pride of the village, and now I was a schoolteacher in the newly built school, a daughter of the soil. I also thought of my younger sister. I was the breadwinner, and I had so many plans for my family. Should I, could I, embark on this course that the forces seemed to be propelling me toward? I knew death could come anytime, but I thought that since I'd had no say in my coming, it was not for me to decide when I leave.

I believed in destiny, just as a person could read another's palm and tell him of his life and when he would accomplish what, how many children he would have, etc. This had to be what was foreordained for me, and therefore my life had already been mapped out. And if I had to die by fire, I would not die by drowning; therefore, I was going to live until I died. I sought God's guidance; I was ready. The words of Mao Tse-tung, like a mantra, kept coming to mind: "Wherever death may surprise us, let it be welcome. If our battle cry has reached even one receptive ear and another hand reaches out to take up our arms …"

6

URBAN GUERRILLA

Two of the brothers from Fyzabad, Michael Lewis and Rodney "Reds" Noel, subsequently visited me at home. They supplied information on the state of affairs for the Fyzabad unit and were introduced to a couple of the brothers from our unit. We grew very close, and they seemed impressed with the way we functioned, so whenever there was a conflict, they would approach me to mediate or give advice.

In celebration of the forty days following Hillary Valentine's death, there was a get-together at his home that included brothers from Diego Martin, Fyzabad, Saint James, Point Fortin, and other areas. African dancing, chanting, drumming, and cooking on three stones were among the activities. The love and camaraderie exhibited was unbelievable. It was like nothing I had experienced before.

I was subsequently given the responsibility for financially coordinating the south. For the women whose men were on the run, as well as for the children and other dependents, my job was to ensure that the children went to school, the rents were paid, and there was food in the household. I also facilitated meetings and so forth. Among the people I helped were Merlin, Barbara, and Sandra. There were others too.

When a new unit was to be formed at Siparia Road, I was asked to orient the six recruits. They were not to be given too much information about the organization, having been told that the less they knew, the safer it would be for them. I informed them that our main interest was not in numbers, since a chain is only as strong as its weakest link. Two solid members were more effective than twenty-two with one weak link. Security was our watchword. The cell structure had to be strictly enforced to limit infiltration.

Following that meeting and induction, Michael and I were unable to find transport to take me back to Point Fortin since the meeting had ended very late that night. I had to work the next day. Michael suggested that I sleep at his home and travel early the next morning. That night while I was lying next to Michael on his bed, we talked about the units, common problems, the recruits, the way forward, etc., until sleep came. I awoke the next morning to see Michael entering the room with a toothbrush and toothpaste, informing me that breakfast was ready. He had earned my respect as a brother. I loved him dearly from then on.

Fyzabad was the home of Tubal Uriah "Buzz" Butler, the militant trade union leader who had migrated to Trinidad from Grenada to work in the oil industry. He mobilized and organized the workers in their fight for better salaries and working conditions. Although he had little education, what he lacked in intellectual ability, he made up for by his use of quotations from the Bible.

Charlie King Junction had been named after a policeman who was set on fire by protestors when he tried to arrest Butler. Fyzabad, which was made up of mainly unemployed and working-class people, was known for its militant trade unionism. Therefore, it was no surprise that a large number of Fyzabad's young men were conscious and gravitated toward the liberation struggle.

I remember being approached by a member of the Youth Forces and Working-Class Movement, of which I was still a member, with the request that I infiltrate Fyzabad. I was told that there were men on the block, dressed in army-type boots, looking very militant but remaining silent. The brothers suspected that these men were on to something "heavy," meaning serious, but they could not get any information from them. One thing they were sure of was that they had not given up the struggle. I remained silent and then changed the topic.

I was told of the two sisters Jennifer and Beverly Jones, whom Johnny greatly admired. He told me of their leaving home very early in the mornings under the guise of going on field trips with their schools when they were engaging in guerilla activities. They were very conscious and brave.

I later came to know the Kaylor family from Diego Martin. They were made up of a mother and father, four beautiful girls, and three boys. One of the girls, who worked as a nurse at the time, reminded me of Angela Davis since they were both fair-skinned and wore large Afros. The youngest girl appeared to be about sixteen years of age. The whole family supported the struggle in many different ways, including renting apartments and cooking for and housing the brothers. Since these brothers and sisters were based in the north of Trinidad, we did not have much direct contact.

On another visit to the Village Council Street "pad" or safe house, I met a roomful of casualties, brothers who for one reason or another could not at that time endure the rigorous treks over the mountains of the Northern Range and therefore were either in the process of obtaining medical care or recuperating from injuries or illnesses.

This was my initial meeting with a brother whom I had heard a lot about. He was fair-skinned with brown hair, was bearded, and had eyes that seemed to be looking through me. He was Terrence "Tuku" Thornhill and was suffering from asthma. His smile revealed a space between his front teeth. He was to later affect my life in a very profound way. Nathaniel "Camillo" Jack, another occupant of the room, had fallen off a ridge and was suffering from an injury to his back. He was a stocky, dark Dougla (a mixture of Afro- and Indo-Trinidadian) with a large Afro hairstyle. I took an instant liking to him. He seemed very humble and down-to-earth in his manner and disposition. One of the brothers, Daniel "Thou" Thomas, whom I had previously met at Bushe Street, had suffered a snakebite after stepping in a snake hole. Brian Jeffers was suffering from ingrown toenails and had difficulty wearing his boots. There was also Johnny with his wounds.

I had often heard references made to Brian Jeffers as the "comandante" with his militant, fearless, no-nonsense moves, which enabled him to escape from extremely difficult encounters with the police. I was meeting him also for the first time. He was tall, well-built, brown-skinned, and extremely handsome. He was also closely associated with the soldiers of the Trinidad and Tobago Defense Force who had mutinied during the 1970 Black Power revolution and was from Saint James's Block Four.

Block Four morphed into the Western Union Liberation Front (WULF), which was made up of unemployed youths from Saint James and members of the Defense Force following the failed attempted mutiny. This is the group from which "the organization" was spawned.

The weapons they had among them were a sawed-off shotgun, two .45 revolvers, and a .22 pistol. This was the same one-room apartment that I had dubbed "the suicide pad." My heart had gone out to these young, handsome men who were in the prime of their lives. What were their crimes that they had to be hunted like animals? Was it loving their country and wanting a better life for its people? their hope that people would have a greater share of the economic pie? that each citizen would contribute according to his or her ability and receive according to his or her need? These men could have been partaking in the best that society had to offer, yet they chose to sacrifice themselves for the benefit of the masses. I thought if they were guilty, then so was I.

They were from different revolutionary groups but all had the same motive and objective. The bond between them was so strong that one could feel it. They had all thrown their hats into the ring. I saw them as being selfless and caring and as having the true Christian values I had previously only read about. I now saw these values manifested in these men. That evening I left with a brother, and by nightfall, a new 16-gauge shotgun was added to the arsenal. Johnny hugged it and danced. To me, it was as if he saw it as an extension of life. My resolve to identify with these men and the cause for which they were fighting became greater.

It was Christmas of 1972. Our unit at Point Fortin had invited the brothers in the north to come down to meet our brothers in the south. Most of the previous meetings had been via travel to the north. I had explained our commitment to the struggle to my mother, educating her about slavery and the labor riots, the various struggles, and the fact that this was a continuation. She was not to worry when I left home following the closure of the school on Fridays and then returned home on Monday mornings, when I bathed, changed, and went to work. She understood.

When she was informed of the guerillas' pending visit and was asked to cook for them, she consented gladly. I remember my younger sister, who was then ten years old, taking the food in basins on her head to the house where the brothers stayed. These were all men wanted by the police in connection with revolutionary activities. Over the next few days, the brothers were filtering in and out, being careful not to arouse suspicion. On one of those days, Johnny and Camillo discussed the revolution, claiming that we others were the ones to continue the struggle since they would soon be gone.

On another occasion, while we were alone at the house in which the brothers were staying, Johnny said something to the effect that when the going gets tough, I may not be around. I responded by slapping him; it was a reflex action that I immediately regretted, but I had felt insulted. He responded by looking at me with a very cold expression and walking away. I think I would have been happy if the earth had opened then and swallowed me up. Such was the level of my humiliation. I tried apologizing, to no avail; it was like speaking to a wall. I was devastated. Sometime later, I approached him again, and his response was, "The difference between animals and humans lies in the fact that humans can reason." He needed not say more. I had learned that lesson. Even though I was tempted to say that action breeds reaction and is equal to it, I held my peace.

It was during this period that Johnny and I got married. We shared how we felt about each other and about the struggle. He felt that he had nothing to offer me, none of the luxuries of life; however, I knew that in giving his life to the struggle, he was making the supreme sacrifice. I had witnessed firsthand his level of commitment, his sacrifices, the work he was putting in, and his concern for the people. He had been specially chosen for this part. What more did he need to give me? I also knew that in committing to him, I was committing to his ideals and the liberation struggle. I knew that one or both of us could be dead at any time, but I also knew that our destiny was not in our hands. And anyway, I believe in crossing bridges as they appear.

In our relationship, Johnny reminded me that the people were to be put first, and we were to place each other second and ourselves last. It was the simplest of ceremonies right there in that old house with no rings and with God as our witness. We exchanged vows and sealed them with a kiss. Our word was our bond. That evening, it was as if Johnny was pouring his soul into mine. We talked about the struggle, the challenges, and the different projects. He told me how much he loved Camillo as a brother.

Johnny related that the night when he received the gunshot wound above his eye, Camillo had come to his rescue and found him lying on the ground. He lifted him and carried him to safety, despite Johnny's pleas for Camillo to save himself; he would hear none of it. Camillo lifted Johnny over a fence although he was losing and regaining consciousness. He did not leave until he had taken him to a place of safety where he could get medical attention, among other things. Camillo had put his life on the line for him.

7

BANK ROBBERY

The organization by now was named the National United Freedom Fighters (NUFF). We were, however, being referred to by the police as "bandits," "criminals," "extremists," "revolutionaries," and "guerillas," whichever suited their purpose. A new secret service squad was formed made up of both army and police, who were reading antiguerilla literature and formed joint patrols to go into the Northern Range to flush out the "guerillas."

By now I had become a regular visitor to Shende Street pad, Trou Macaque, Village Council Street, and other places in the north. However, I never divulged my name or my identity. I was known simply as "the sister from the south." Johnny had now grown to trust me and seemed to have confidence in my intuitive abilities. He would seek out my opinion on many issues and discuss my situations and other problems with the brothers. I looked forward to times when I would accompany brothers to meetings, remaining silent while observing body language and assessing people's character and genuineness. I was seldom, if ever, wrong in my assessments. We called this "feeling out" the vibration of the person.

We had once gone on an offensive to liberate some funds for the organization, but that was aborted because civilians would have been in the line of fire if anything had gone wrong. We subsequently retreated to a safe house at Trou Macaque for a postmortem.

Following this, I was told to occupy the only bed in the one-bedroom apartment, while the others bunked on the floor of the living room.

When I awoke the next morning, I saw N in the room. On realizing that the space on the bed next to me was undisturbed, I asked him where he had slept. With a wide grin, he pointed to a straw mat on the floor and explained that mankind had ordered him to sleep in the room. I simply smiled. That was the level of his discipline.

Mankind had rejected the orthodox English language, choosing to speak dialect, even developing our own vocabulary, referring to food as "jawt," the hills as "heights," the houses in the communities as "flats," and each other as "mankind"—while the poor people were "the masses." I viewed this as a way of grounding with the brothers and facilitating communication by removing complexes.

The organization was now expanding rapidly. With units in places such as Woodbrook, Laventille, Tunapuna, Point Fortin, Belmont, Fyzabad, Sangre Grande, Diego Martin, Saint James, Boissierre, Siparia Road, Rio Claro, and San Juan, there was a need for more safe houses, cars, motorbikes, and other forms of transport. In addition, there were more families to be provided for.

The military arm, the ones to go on direct offensives, was increasing, but a great deal of work needed to be undertaken among the people in terms of education, organizing, and planning. Several offensives were engaged to liberate money, while people pooled resources and raised funds, but there came a time when growth was so rapid that there was a need for larger sums of money.

We were discussing this situation at Trou Macaque when Johnny said to me that a major offensive was being contemplated, that too many of mankind were getting involved in minor offensives. The heights men would handle this one. However, there was a need for a female "to cool the scene." My response was, "Look no further: they have one." He was taken aback and wanted to know whether or not I was serious. I simply said, "Uh-huh," meaning yes. He smiled broadly and told me it would be discussed with mankind, who would make the final decision.

About two days later I was summoned. I was given my clothes and a wig and was told of the role I would be required to play in the liberation of the funds from a bank. I was to get one of the tellers away from the counter, get over the counter, empty his till into a money bag, then leave with the others. It was agreed upon. Just a few days before, Jennifer and I were discussing the fact that we were not allowed to go on serious offensives but were just as much at risk as the men if boarded by the police. We had planned to raise this issue at some point in the near future.

Camillo had continued to suffer from back problems since his fall, so it was decided that he and Jennifer would set up a pad at Point Fortin. He was to continue working full time with the brothers, who by now had been working with about twenty-five unemployed youths in the area on another agricultural project. They had begun clearing the land but needed financial assistance. Only a couple of the brothers knew of the connection between this project and the organization. Should there be a protracted war, food would be needed. In addition, there was the work of character-building to be done among the youths.

It was around this time that Johnny asked, "Did you tell Ruth Bayley about the new projects or the upcoming scene?"

"No, I did not," I responded.

"She is not to know any more than she already knows, since she is under investigation. She was seen in the company of two policemen by two sisters who were in the vicinity. She had introduced them to the police officers by their names, which is not in keeping with the clandestine nature of the organization."

He mentioned other incidents that were highly suspicious, such as the fact that Ruth had befriended the sisters and was always asking questions of them. He went on to state that further investigation was needed before any possible confrontation. I was taken aback by this development. I used to admire the way Ruth conducted herself, and I believed that she was one of the founders of the organization. Until then, there had been no occasion for lengthy dialogue between us apart from the exchange of pleasantries.

The evening before the bank robbery, two brothers came to my home to pick me up. I drove to the north after telling a close brother from my unit to listen to the ten o'clock news the next morning. At the Shende Street pad that night, we sat in a circle to discuss the plan for the following day and the dovetailing of the various roles. I sat there, quietly assessing each person in turn, unable to find any weak link. I saw each one as being prepared to sacrifice his life for the common good.

On the morning of February 22, 1973, at around nine o'clock, we drove to the bank in the north. Tuku and I were dropped off a few yards before reaching the bank. We walked down the street arm in arm. He was dressed in a white shirt, a tie, and dress pants, while I was wearing a tangerine-colored two-piece skirt and jacket, a shaggy brownish wig, and large sunglasses. On entering the bank, I walked toward the counter with the deposit slips, pretending to fill one out while waiting for the others to get into their positions.

I was carrying a gun in my skirt pocket, which was covered by my jacket. I then approached my teller and pointed the gun at him, telling him, "Move away from the counter!" He froze. After two sterner commands, he still did not, or could not, move. I called N for assistance, and it was only then that the teller responded. I then proceeded to climb onto the counter. While up there, I saw a woman who pressed a button, which caused a tangerine light to begin flashing. I later learned that she was the accountant. The closest person to me was N. I shouted to him, "She's dialing someone! The light!" He said something to her, then ripped the cord from the wall. I assumed then that the light indicated that the Criminal Investigation Department of the police service had been called, but later I learned that it was the head office of the bank.

All eyes were now on me. I jumped off the counter and proceeded to the till. A money bag was handed to me, and the money from the till was emptied into it.

Two of the employees came to me telling me how frightened they were. I told them that we were guerrillas from the hills and that the money was to be used in the interests of the people. They were to just do as they were told and no harm would come to them. They seemed reassured but kept following me. This hadn't been in the script. I knew the others had emptied the other three tills and collected the money from the vault after herding the customers and security staff into a room. Mankind was now wearing the security officer's uniform and had taken his gun. Propaganda about our identity and objectives, in the form of pamphlets, was distributed at the bank as we made our exit.

While leaving the bank, I was sitting in the back seat of one of the employees' cars next to the accountant with two of mankind at the front. The others were in the manager's car with the manager as we made our escape. We drove a short distance away and then released the hostages. On reaching our cars, I changed my clothes and left them, along with the wig and other items, in one of the cars.

"Ya going back to the house?" one of mankind inquired.

"No. I'll go to work. I'll check you all sometime later," was my response.

I was dropped off at a point where I could get transport to Port of Spain, then I traveled by taxi to Point Fortin. On the way down, there was a news flash on the car radio that four men and a woman, in what was described as a "daring robbery," had robbed a bank in the north of the island. It was the largest bank robbery in the history of the country. An island-wide manhunt had been launched in Trinidad.

Everything went more or less as planned except for a few minor hitches. I was smiling on the inside. I went straight to work. That evening, on my return home from school, I was greeted by Chipo, who was wearing a broad grin. He too had been listening to the news. We talked briefly.

One of my close brothers, Treve, came up asking me, "Where did you go last night?" At the same time, he smiled knowingly, then continued, saying, "You have to be the person referred to in story about the bank robbery that was on the news this morning."

"I don't know what you are talking about." I feigned ignorance. We both smiled and went our respective ways.

None of the other members of the unit were informed. I retreated to my bedroom and dressed down to my undergarments, then lay across my bed reliving and evaluating the events of the day.

I neither saw nor heard my mother enter the room, but when I came out of my reverie, there she stood looking at me with a very solemn expression as if she had been weeping. "It is you," she said, reminding me that I had left the night before. "Tell me,"

she implored, "so that I will know what to do in case of trouble!" She went on, saying, "From the time I heard the news, I knew it was you. I could not work. I had to leave."

"What are you talking about?" I asked, pretending not to know what she was speaking about, and admonishing her to be careful of her utterances falling on the wrong ears. She insisted that I tell her the truth. I smilingly told her that she was worrying too much, then left to go to the shop for an evening newspaper. At this point, I believe she was crying. I could not lie to her.

Chipo and a few of the brothers who were involved in our agricultural project were transplanting lettuce, tomatoes, and other seedlings close to my home. I called out to him, and we left on foot for the nearest newspaper stand, which was about ten minutes away. Once there, we began reading the evening newspaper. He was joking about the contents of the article on the bank robbery, which read that "the chick moved cool and businesslike," while on our way back.

As we approached the house, another brother pulled up in a vehicle. He was extremely agitated. "I just heard a news flash, and there is a gun battle taking place right now between police and guerillas in a house at Trou Macaque. Some of them are dead." There was to be a report on the seven o'clock evening news. Chipo and I looked at each other. We did not speak. My stomach somersaulted, and my legs became very weak. We hurried to the house and waited for what seemed like an eternity without speaking.

As the news came on, my worst nightmares were confirmed. I recognized two of the four dead bodies: Johnny and Camillo. The other two I could not identify at the time. One turned out to be Ulric Gransaul, who was attached to the San Juan block, and the other was Mervyn "Blancs" Belgrave from Fyzabad. My younger sister also recognized the former two. My mother let out a heart-wrenching, "O God, why did you go? Why? Why?" A million thoughts were racing through my mind. *How? Who? Who was the weak link?* I tried not to display my emotions. The show had to go on. Reality had stepped in. I was now on the run. I placated my mother as best I could, telling her I wouldn't be sleeping at home that night; managed to put some clothes and other items together; and kissed her and my sister, promising to return the next day or keep in touch, depending on how the situation developed.

The driver, Chipo, Treve, and I left for a safe house at Point Fortin. We went there directly and waited. It was a most agonizing night. I tossed and turned for the greater part, trying to find comfort in sleep, but sleep was a torturous enemy. Still uncertain of what had transpired, I pondered the next move while awaiting news concerning the latest developments. I was not identified in the morning newspaper.

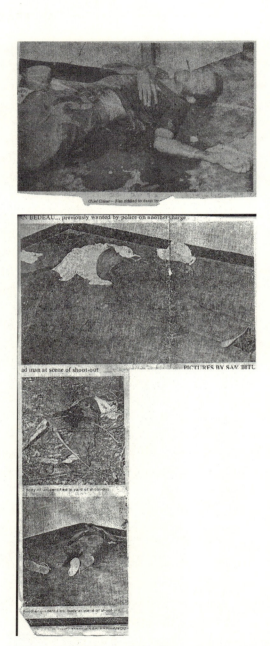

Bodies of four freedom fighters killed by police at a house at Trou Macaque following a bank robbery on February 22, 1973. *Top:* John Bedeau. *Center:* Nathaniel Jack, Mervyn Belgrave, and Ulric Gransaul.

I visited my mother and sister that evening. My mother implored me to go to Venezuela through the back door. I jokingly told her, "The struggle is here. Why must I run away?" I was thinking all the while that mankind could have been knocked out with tear gas and captured, but I remembered their conversations about the messages sent to them by the head of the Flying Squad and other senior police officers that anytime they came face-to-face with them, they would be dead men. *They have certainly made good on their threats*, I thought.

After I left home, I visited a couple of the other brothers to inform them of my new status. Two of them wanted to go on the run with me, but I disapproved, reminding them of the amount of work still to be done among the people. "We are still a long way from liberation morning," I opined. Leaving some instructions concerning the future functioning of the unit, I contacted some people, being careful not to get in touch with anyone from NUFF.

The next day, accompanied by Treve, I went to see Michael Als. He was hosting a conference at a beach house in the south. I sent a message indicating that I needed to speak with him urgently. He immediately came outside and greeted us warmly.

"Have you heard the latest news concerning a bank robbery?" I asked him.

"Yes, I have," he responded.

After a long pause, not meeting his questioning gaze, I informed him, "I happen to be the woman whom the police are searching for. I need your help."

He was astonished and stood speechless, shifting his gaze from Treve to me in a questioning manner. He seemed bewildered, as if unable to process the magnitude of what I had said. I went on to provide him with a little more detail. His initial response was to hug me tightly and protectively. When he had found his voice he said, "I am proud of you, my sister. You had the key to this corrupt society in your hands, you and all the others like you, yet you have turned your backs on it and have chosen to fight for this cause. I will protect you. You are very brave, sister. Go to my mother's house and tell her that I have sent you and that she is to let you stay in my room. I will be there as soon as I can." I went to his home accompanied by Treve.

The next morning, I received a call from Treve, who had returned home that night.

"Endless police at your mother's house!"

"Do not call back! Stay low, and take care. Keep the faith. Don't worry, I'll be OK," I responded.

I subsequently informed Michael of the latest development, letting him know that I had to move at once. That very day I was relocated. Michael ensured that I did not have to stay too long in any one place. I still did not make any effort to contact NUFF. His brothers were of great assistance. Even his youngest sister was very supportive.

8

ON THE RUN

For Carnival that year, 1973, I was at the home of a Caucasian couple who lived in the northwest of Trinidad. Acquaintances of Michael, they had gone abroad, leaving me to occupy the servants' quarters while their foreign Caucasian guest stayed at the house. I had my daily newspapers, and fresh fruits were brought each day. In addition, I had access to a well-stocked refrigerator. The greater portion of my time was spent in my room reading and sleeping.

After about eleven days, I returned to the south dressed in a nurse's uniform. The taxi driver, on nearing San Fernando General Hospital, tried on several occasions to ask me where I was getting off. I had not gotten used to my identity as a nurse. On realizing I was the center of attention, I quickly apologized, stating that I had been lost in thought and daydreaming, which the other occupants of the car found to be quite amusing.

I had only arrived at my destination about five minutes prior and had just taken off my uniform and wig when someone exclaimed, "Police! Through the back!" I dashed through the back of the house after dressing hastily, then I climbed a wire fence and found my way to the front of the hospital, where I hid under a bus shed, uncertain of my next move. The police station was a few yards away. Police were driving by in droves, and I was somewhat confused.

I waited. A car stopped a short distance from where I stood, and I was signaled to come. Seated in the back seat was Michael.

It was a taxi. Our communication was coded. He told me where I should get off and the house number without speaking directly to me. He remained in the car when I got out, and the driver drove off. It was not until more than forty years later that I found out who was responsible for that leak.

The owner of the house was awaiting my arrival at Pond Road La Romain. He did not ask too many questions, about which I was happy. I remained there for about one week before being moved to another location. This brother lived alone. I'll call him Len. I was introduced as Pat. While I was there, some of my worst fears materialized. Despite all the newspaper headlines I was making and all the propaganda that was being published, no picture of me had as yet appeared in any of the newspapers. I had taken care to get rid of all the photographs that I had at home. I had even visited the police station to determine which brothers had bounties on their heads.

Up to that time, I had felt relatively safe. However, that very day, my picture appeared in the evening newspaper. It had been obtained from the driving school where I was seeking to obtain my driver's permit. I and a few other NUFF members were now wanted dead or alive with a ten-thousand-dollar bounty on our heads. Things were getting warm. It was time to move.

I remembered a half-Chinese friend of Len who did some very conscious drawings. I knew he was a genuine brother by the vibes that emanated from his artwork. This was enough to convince me. The next day during his visit, I revealed my identity to him and explained why I needed to remain on neutral territory. That very evening, he took me to his home and showed me how to gain access should we not be able to establish contact when or if the need arose. Little did I know that my faith in Len was to be tested the very next day.

It was late evening. I had just had a bath and was now walking across the street from Len's, where there was a school, when a car pulled up with a driver and another person, who was seated in the front passenger seat. Len was seated in the back. He told me they were going to check on someone and inquired whether I wanted to accompany them. I got into the back seat. We stopped once to enable me to get an orange drink. It turned out the person was not at home, so we began returning to Len's house. This took about twenty minutes.

On approaching the house, I noticed there was an unusually large number of people on the street. As we got closer, I realized that policemen, armed to the teeth with self-loading rifles and submachine guns, had surrounded Len's house. They were inside and outside the house, which was on a lower level than the road. All the lights were turned on. We were above, looking into the house. As the driver slowed down, a little girl came to the car, saying, "Police looking for Pat."

Realizing that Len was speechless, probably in shock, I said, "They are probably searching Len for marijuana. Driver, let's go back out to the road." The driver obeyed what could have been interpreted as a command.

As we neared the intersection at the major road, we could see and hear vehicles revving and coming after us. Ahead I saw my newfound half-Chinese friend, whom I'll refer to as Chinee, signaling us to stop. I told the driver to pick him up, which he did. He had been waiting to intercept us, but we had not returned the way we had left. He took charge and directed the driver to turn left, then right, as was necessary to evade the police, who were hot on our heels.

Eventually, we succeeded. Chinee subsequently took us to an older army man's house, where we both got out, the other occupants of the car being advised to return to Len's house to avoid being deemed wanted men or being beaten by the police. They were free to say whatever came to their minds. The soldier was not at home, but I knew that we had to leave there as soon as possible. I requested from his wife a change of clothing and changed my hairstyle from Nubian knots to an Afro, following which Chinee and I set out on foot. I started with the premise that mankind would talk under pressure. We couldn't take any chances.

Chinee and I were hugging, pretending to be lovers. Each time the lights from the cars flashed, I laughingly buried my face in his chest. This went on for a while until we came to another army man's house who was to go on a trip early the next morning. It was a two-apartment house with one toilet. The owner locked the door from the outside to avoid suspicion since his neighbor knew he would be out for the day. Chinee was to return to his home since we were unsure whether or not he had been recognized.

Chinee was also to make some contacts. I was alone and had to ensure that I aroused no suspicion that someone was in the house. I put on a pair of socks and had to negotiate the use of the washroom and also ensure that I refrained from sneezing, coughing, or dropping anything.

About a month after that fateful day, it was time to leave the south. The next day, contact was established with a brother from the north and arrangements were made for me to go to his house. I traveled by taxi. He was not at home. I told his mother that I was a friend and would await his return. He was the leader of another revolutionary organization who, I subsequently learned, had just returned from Cuba. On seeing me sitting quietly in his room on his return, he was astonished, accusing me of being a spy who had been planted in his house. I remained calm and composed, requesting something to eat. He turned the lights out and went to the kitchen even though I had been in his room all day. On his return, he continued to interrogate me about NUFF, asking who its leader was, how it was run, etc. I told him that I only knew as much as I needed to know and that he would be safer if he adopted that policy. Then I told him only as much as I felt that he needed to know.

That night, as I lay on the end of his waterbed, I could smell the alcohol on his breath. I lay on my back reflecting on the events of the day. I then felt the touch of his hand, trying to draw me closer to him. I relaxed and did not resist as he gently pulled me over. I calmly got up and sat cross-legged on the bed, then got up, put on the light, went back to my original position on the bed, and asked, "Where is your revolutionary discipline?" I was looking at him straight in the eye without fear and with much calm.

"Nothing is wrong with my action, I being male and you being female."

"My thinking is that there should be mutual consent." He remained silent. "Mankind does not take too kindly to this kind of behavior. You could be shot or killed for taking advantage of a sister who is seeking the assistance of a fellow revolutionary."

"I am sorry. I was out with friends and had a few drinks earlier today, hence the reason for my inappropriate behavior."

I accepted his apology. He returned to his end of the bed, and I had a peace-filled night. Early the next morning, he went to contact some people for me. By nightfall I was on a minibus accompanied by a brother from NUFF, on my way to my new safe house.

It turned out that I was taken to this brother's home, where I was introduced as his girlfriend, a postal worker on vacation. I spent about a week there. His family was made up of his mother, brothers, and sisters. We attended meetings and other activities in his unit. After about a week, his real girlfriend got wind that there was another woman at his home, so the scene was now too hot for me. I moved to another brother, who lived with his wife and family. It was while I was there that I visited Ruth at her home. Arrangements were made for me to see my mother and stepfather, who were brought up to spend the day with me. I was overjoyed to see my mother again. She appeared calm and relieved that at least physically I was all right. We chatted about the other members of the family and the latest developments in the village, among other things. Ruth did an excellent job as the host. I was still finding it hard to believe that she could be guilty of being an informer. I was watching her every move.

There had been a recent police murder, and Brian Jeffers was staying in the garage of Ruth's home, seemingly until things had quieted down. Ruth had subsequently gone up to the heights or into the hills. It was around this time that arrangements were made for me to go to the hills or heights to see the brothers I had not seen since that fateful day about three months prior. I was taken up by night and was overjoyed to see them all: Kenneth, Tenia, Tuku, Jaiye, Jeff, Clemey, Guy, and others. Clemey had come up that same night while Ruth had gone down. We talked about my activities over the past three months.

Ruth had been accused of informing. There had been a trial, and she was released based on insufficient evidence and a dream that was had by Guy Harewood, one of the leaders of NUFF. That evening, while sitting in a cross-legged position, facing Tuku and talking with him, I had a vision of Johnny and Camillo. It was around six o'clock in the evening, and they were both dressed in familiar clothing, N in a blue shirt with sleeves rolled up to his elbows, and Camillo in a black jersey and jeans. They were coming toward us and talking animatedly with each other. Suddenly, I could neither talk nor move. I remained transfixed. It was only after they had passed that I was able to talk and move. When I recounted my experience to Tuku, he suggested that what I had seen was their astral bodies.

I was to return to the flats early the next morning about five o'clock so that the brothers could "prowl" early. The time came and went, but transport did not arrive. Something was amiss. Anxiety was setting in. Then someone was spotted coming up the river at about eight in the morning. It was Freddy from the Fyzabad unit. He reported that plan A had to be canceled. Ruth had gone directly to the police upon leaving the camp, and sixteen persons by their count had been arrested that morning. We had to move on.

I was unprepared both mentally and physically for what lay ahead. I was given a pair of boots, some socks, and a knapsack with supplies, and after a couple of days a hammock, which was regarded as an extremely precious commodity since most slept on the bare earth. The menu that day was dumplings and corned beef. My appetite was poor. I gave my food away. Everyone had similar portions. That night I was to regret this act, as after walking all day, sleep would not come. I was weary, fatigued, and hungry. While lying gazing at the stars, I sat up, only to realize that Clemey was also awake.

"Are you all right?" he asked.
"I am extremely hungry."
"I have a similar problem."

We decided to investigate our knapsacks and discovered that there were bowls, milk, and sugar. We used water from our canteens to make what we called a "gash," which we drank and then went to sleep.

The following morning, we were greeted by Jeff, who asked, "How all yuh spent the night?" We began relating our experiences with hunger. Jeff listened attentively, asked a few questions, and then with a smile unexpectedly summoned the others.

"Mankind, come and hear this." At this point, he asked us to repeat what we had told him after they had gathered around. I was a bit confused at this stage as to his motive, but I cautiously went along. Clemey unsuspectingly repeated what he had said to Jeff earlier.

There were exclamations such as, "Eh, heh?"; "What!"; and "Really?"

It was not until the end of our interrogation that we were informed by Jeff, "What y'all did was against the rules, as the contents of our knapsacks are communal property." The knapsacks contained basic survival items, and the contents of each were similar. If any knapsack got left behind while making a hasty retreat, or if anyone perished along the way, then essential supplies would still be available.

We were facing the people's court, consisting all the brothers in camp. We were tried, and a verdict of guilty was handed down. The penalty was also agreed upon, which was that we were both to go on a water prowl down the very steep ridge to the nearby river with all available water canteens, which we were to fill and return. In addition, we were to do extra guard duty. Guy Harewood had volunteered to stay up with me since it was my first guard duty experience. This was my baptism of fire. I had learned my lesson.

The following days were rough. Upon tripping on a vine, I twisted my ankle and began falling down a steep ridge. The only thing to stem my descent was a sandbox tree characterized by long "pickers," or spikes, that punctured the palms of my hands. Hot water and balm were placed on my swollen ankle, which did not do much to quell the pain, but I tried not to complain. I always started the prowl or our treks over the mountains as second or third in line, but always ended up last. Jaiye and the others would take turns staying behind with me. For twelve hours each day, we prowled the Northern Range to our destination. On one occasion, a large Tigre snake crossed our path. We all stopped and remained very still in our tracks until it went on its way. It was my first encounter with such a large reptile. Another time we had to throw our knapsacks over and crawl under a fallen tree trunk. The fresh scent of a reptile permeated the atmosphere. I simply prayed that I would not see it.

A bath was a luxury. I hadn't had one in two weeks. My most memorable and fearsome experience was early one morning when it was still pitch-black out. Dogs were heard barking. They were getting closer and closer to the camp. My first thought was of the police. All were awakened and told to "back" or go behind a tree. This we did. Although one of the brothers stood next to me, I was petrified. I did not know the terrain and wondered what predicament I would find myself in if I were to get lost and be separated from the group. The barking of the dogs drew nearer and nearer until it began fading in the distance. I simply remained silent. It was the first time I had experienced fear. The intruders turned out to be hunters.

I developed severe back pains, and it was decided that I should go down before the next offensive, which was now in the planning stage. My inability to keep up with the prowling, coupled with the thought of going back down to the flats, made me feel both vulnerable and unsafe. My heart was heavy and I was dejected, but I knew that what we were doing was for the common good.

After two weeks, we returned to our starting point. On our return journey, as we were nearing the camp, I felt that I could not take another step. Tuku stayed back with me, urging me on. He carried both our knapsacks and gave me a cutlass to hold. Even that felt as if it weighed a ton. My frustration and despair grew to the point that I threw the cutlass down a ridge. Tuku simply looked at me with his piercing brownish-gray eyes told me to hang on. Then he went back down the ridge, retrieved the cutlass, and waited until I was ready to go. "We're almost there," he said. I cannot describe how I felt. I was ashamed.

We had to walk up the river, which was a risky business. I knew that Tuku was risking his life by staying back with me. He never once got angry, although he was exhausted. Once we reached the camp, the others slowly clapped us in. I don't remember Tuku telling them about the cutlass. I began to appreciate the brothers more, my respect and admiration growing. I was both happy and sad to go down. I could not make the prowl, yet I felt that life in the flats was more unpredictable than in the heights. I vowed to continue the work with greater zeal, reading, making hammocks, attending meetings, collecting newspaper clippings, and encouraging the faithful.

A new pad was acquired at Saint Joseph where brothers from the south were allowed to visit. However, not many people were to know of my whereabouts. It was while I was there that I had a vision of a man entering the room and angrily looking at me one night while I was lying on the top bunk of the bed. I knew that I had not been asleep and was having an experience similar to the one I had when I saw the vision of Johnny and Camillo, with neither being able to move or speak, as this man came through the window, which was closed, and approached me.

It turned out that he was the deceased father of the owner of the house, who frequented the place when the time came for his prayers, which were to be kept but were delayed. I would see him day or night. Although I understood neither the meaning of nor the reason for these visions, I simply felt that my spirit was making contact with another dimension and was never fearful when they occurred. They somehow served to strengthen my faith in God.

One evening I had visitors from both the north and the south who had not seen me for a while and wanted to remain for some time. I urged them not to stay the night since this would be safer for them. The other person who was supposed to be there that night had been called out to work a double shift. As fate would have it, the next morning, to my horror, the police arrived.

As I came to the end of my reverie, with no idea of how long I had been in that room, the thought struck me: *Is this a trap geared toward enticing me to escape? Why am I not handcuffed? Why are there no guards in the room? Will I be shot, possibly killed, for attempting to escape from police custody if I venture out of the room?* I remained seated.

My now-growing level of anxiety was then abated by the reappearance of Mr. Burroughs, the head of the Flying Squad, a special police unit formed in 1970 after the Black Power uprisings, which became famous for its relentless pursuit of those associated with the National United Freedom Fighters. Mr. Burroughs had his signature self-loading rifle in one hand, and in the other was his cap and a small towel. Lowering his gaze while slowly shaking his head from side to side, he began wiping the mouth of his weapon with the towel. He displayed a sad countenance while speaking in a very apologetic tone.

"Jay, I am very sorry for the way things turned out, but I had no control over what just took place. We got a tip-off: there was a shootout. Both Guy Harewood and Brian Jeffers are dead." He was almost tearful in expressing his sorrow about the seemingly tragic events,

"You were lucky. Those boys could have been my sons. We did not mean to kill them, but we had no choice." He continued apologizing profusely. It was then that I broke down crying. I felt as if my world had come crashing down around me. To say that I was distraught is an understatement. I began processing what could have possibly transpired to result in the death of those two brothers, who were regarded as leaders of the organization, as well as in my capture, all in the same morning. Little did I know that morning that this was all part of Mr. Burroughs' intimidating theatrics.

9

INTERROGATION

If what I just described in chapter 8 was a bad dream, then what followed was my worst nightmare. I was left sitting in that room for as long as I can remember. I spent the night sitting on a straight chair. The next day I was taken to an upstairs room in which about eight men were seated. Mr. Burroughs was not present. I was given a chair on which to sit, and they began shooting questions at me. One with a husky voice, Toppin, was the main aggressor. "Where is X? Where do you all meet? Where do you pass to go up to the hills?" Initially, I remained silent. Then they began shouting menacingly. Toppin was pounding on the desk. I began denying knowledge of his accusations, claiming that I was from the south and knew neither the northern people nor the terrain. This went on for what seemed like hours.

I realized that they were fabricating a story. At one point when I said that I did not know a particular person, I noticed that Toppin wrote that I did know the person. I pointed this out, stating that he was writing things that I did not say. He responded by saying that I should mind my business and answer the questions since what he was writing had nothing to do with me.

The interrogation continued until well into the night. The police were shouting at times, and sometimes banging on the desk. I was in pain, tired, exhausted, and sleepy. It was like a question-and-answer session with them filling in the blank spaces. Questions were coming from every direction. I remembered the brothers who had been tortured by them, so I decided to admit to knowing John Bedeau and accompanying him on the bank robbery. I feigned ignorance of all else, thereby protecting the others.

When I refused to say anything further, a file about three inches thick consisting of sheets of typewritten paper was brought in. This was later referred to by mankind as "the gospel according to Ruth." The police read from this file of my encounters with NUFF involving Ruth, mentioning details about our first meeting, the clothes I was wearing, my headscarf, the names of occupants of the car, the color, make, and license plate number of the car, and even the names of the books that were given to me. They continued in this manner, turning pages and reading to me, punctuating everything with a sarcastic, "You do not know?" while asking me if I thought that I was fooling big men. Everything included the minutest details.

Years later I learned that Ruth Bayley, following her trial in the heights, had gone straight to the police for protection. She was kept at the police barracks for several months. There she wrote her UWI exams and was subsequently given a scholarship and asylum in England in exchange for all the information she had about NUFF.

I was taken back downstairs very late that night and had to sit on a chair all night. The next day I was taken back to the room, where I was shown a few lines on a piece of white paper that I was told to sign. I was also presented with sheets of typewritten paper on which places were identified where I should place my initials and sign. I protested vehemently, saying that I did not know what was written on those sheets of paper. I told the police that if I wanted to give a statement, then I was quite capable of writing it. I kept repeating that I had not given them a statement and continued to refuse to sign the papers. They were now shouting angrily. One of them, with clenched fists, lunged at me, shouting, "Gim mih ah chance with she. Leh mih ram mih hand in she neck," while two others restrained him.

Another said, "We will put her in a cell with Theresa."

Another, in agreement, stated, "She doh want to sign? When

Theresa finish with she, she will be on her hands and knees begging to sign." Then they went on to explain that Theresa was a policewoman with an elongated part of her sexual anatomy, a lesbian and karate expert who was greatly feared by all her victims. I asked to speak to a lawyer.

They responded by asking me, "Who said that you needed a lawyer?" They said they recognized that my innocence had been taken advantage of, and therefore they had already contacted my mother so that I could go home as soon as I signed the papers. I was now thinking of the many NUFF members who had been detained, tortured and beaten while in police custody, including Beverly Jones, who had been held and charged with possession of ammunition and marijuana before she jumped bail and went up to the heights.

The police were so vicious and unpredictable that I began to wonder if anyone knew that I was in custody. They could quite easily say that I tried to escape and shoot me. I rationalized that robbery was a bailable offense, and therefore I would sign the papers. If charged, I would jump bail and return to the hills. With this in mind, I signed the sixteen places they commanded me to sign, protesting each time I had to do so, and was subsequently told that there was a place where I could take all my complaints.

After my appearance before a justice of the peace, I was taken to a police cell, where I spent the night on a board measuring eight feet by four feet. There was a filthy commode with no cover in the center of the cell, and I could hear the prisoners in the other cells calling out to each other, and to me, telling me to stay up and be strong. The next morning, sometime after eight o'clock, I was taken to Golden Grove Women's Prison. The entourage consisted of a police jeep at the front, one carrying a matron and me, followed by other vehicles with fully armed police.

On arrival at Golden Grove Women's Prison, I saw the first gate at the entrance, followed by another gate, followed by yet another, before entering the one leading directly to the women's prison. There was an asphalt-paved yard bordered by a lawn with neat rows of well-tended flowers.

A short, dark, plump elderly woman with curved legs and of African descent was there as part of the welcoming committee. I subsequently learned that she was the matron of the women's prison. I was led up about five steps to a long veranda with a waxed wooden floor, then into a passageway of what appeared to be an old wooden colonial barrack-type building painted cream and green, complete with mesh wire windows. I passed what appeared to be offices on one side of a passageway. We subsequently entered a room where I was made to strip off all my clothing and undergo a most embarrassing and invasive body search. It was for me the most humiliating deed I have ever performed. Little did I know that this was only the beginning of a ritual to be performed once one left the compound of the prison and returned. I protested and I cried, to no avail.

In the end, I was led through a narrow passageway to a backyard where there was a long table with benches on either side, with two large concrete washing sinks. A drain separated the sinks from what I learned was the cellblock, which consisted of three cells in a row with a toilet and bathroom opposite the last one. This block was fenced with concrete and wire. I was placed in the middle cell. The furniture consisted of a bunk, a potty, and what looked like a thousand-watt bulb hanging from the ceiling. I was given an enamel jug of water, and the heavy doors, which made a thunderous sound when slammed, were slammed behind me. The officer with a huge bunch of keys ensured that I was locked in. It all seemed like a dream.

The next morning, cold reality hit me at around four o'clock, when I was awakened by the turnkeys to get my morning bath, empty my potty, and replenish my water. Around three o'clock in the afternoon, I was taken out of the cellblock for a one-hour airing. All the prisoners had to be out of sight and hearing range. I was escorted to the place close to the kitchen with officers doing surveillance, an area known as the labor yard.

The Black Maria or prison on wheels, police cars, and jeeps provided transport to and from the court. These were accompanied by numerous escorts. Getting out of this place was all that occupied my mind. I felt that once the brothers were out there, they would never allow us to stay in prison. My thoughts were frequently on those who died, those in prison, and the ones on the outside. *Where do we go from here?* I looked forward to going to court, but I dreaded the return and having to submit to those unorthodox searches. My days were spent sleeping, rendering it difficult to sleep at night with the bright bulb overhead. Following the hearing in the lower magistrate court, I was committed to stand trial in the high court. No bail was granted.

Communication with the brothers was difficult, as was accessing news from the outside. I was isolated. Special officers were chosen to sit between my visitors and me, while others stood close by. I stayed clear of anyone associated with NUFF.

At the time of my arrest, six NUFF members had already been shot dead by the police, three were imprisoned for bank robbery and other arms and ammunition-related charges, and one, David Michael, had been tortured and framed for the murder of a policeman. Scores of our members were questioned, some of them being beaten and released.

Despite their propaganda, the police didn't know much about the operation of the organization at this stage. The murder of John Bedeau and the others was a major blow to NUFF. Another fatal wound was the defection of Ruth Bayley with the vital information which she fed to the police.

Because of the clandestine nature of the organization, how the organization evolved, and the limited knowledge that members had, most did not know of each other or of other people's roles for security reasons. I knew then that polarization would set in. It was just a matter of time. Not enough work had been done concerning the education of the cells or the people. The first publication identifying the organization, stating its aims and objectives and claiming responsibility for its offensives against the state, had been distributed at the bank during the robbery. More were to hit the street that night, but in most cases, the distribution had to be aborted because the police were highly vigilant.

By the end of my first six months on remand, three more brothers were arrested on murder charges, while countless others had been held and interrogated. Three policemen had been killed, and three more NUFF members, including seventeen-year-old Beverly Jones, had now been killed by the police following an ambush in the Northern Range. An eyewitness, in his account, stated as follows:

> From the top of the ridge, we heard, "Drop your guns!" and the soldiers opened fire. Everybody dropped to the ground, and again there was an exchange of fire. During this exchange, I looked around and saw Beverly was wounded. She got a bullet to the side of her face, which had taken off the skin. You could see her teeth. She was also shot in her leg. Another comrade, Kenneth Tenia, was going to crawl over a log, and he was shot in the head and died instantly. Beverly ran down the hill with some others and started asking for water. When they got to the river, they heard cracking in the bushes, so they took her up and ran with her. Six or seven times they ran and rested. The last time, Terrence Thornhill and another brother told her to lie down and covered her with a green blanket to camouflage her. Out of nowhere, soldiers appeared, shooting. The brothers didn't have time to pick her up, and the soldiers killed her right there under the blanket.

Beverly's then nineteen-year-old sister Jennifer and several others were by now in custody on charges ranging from sabotage, to robbery, to possession of arms and ammunition, to shooting with intent. This occurred following a more than twelve-hour-long gun battle with police and more than four hundred soldiers in the forested hills of the Northern Range. It is believed that this all resulted from a tip-off by the brother of one of the guerillas. He, I was told, was subsequently executed by mankind.

JUNE 1, 1973

Among the offensives engaged in by NUFF was the attack on a tropospheric scatter station valued at more than two million dollars at the time. The main objective of this effort was to ambush the police during their response, so that much-needed arms and ammunition could be obtained. Four policemen were injured, but the mission had failed mainly because the police possessed superior weapons.

AUGUST 7, 1973

Six bags of ammunition, eight shotguns, a pistol, and a revolver were liberated by four armed guerrillas from a firearms dealer and hardware proprietor in the south. Simultaneously, on August 7, 1973, thirteen shotguns and one handgun were liberated from the Matelot police station in the north by guerrillas.

Terrence Thornhill, in whose company I had entered the bank, had been arrested and was facing twenty-five charges. He was captured on the same day Guy Harewood was killed. Merlyn Wright and two other sisters from Fyzabad had also passed through the prison, providing me with updates on the situation in the south. My hopes of being freed from prison had dwindled since most of the key members of NUFF were either on the defensive or in prison, or had been killed. The relentless pressure placed on the organization by the police resulted in the spawning of informers, three of whom were allegedly killed by mankind.

By this time, because of pressure from newspaper articles and other forms of protest, I was now allowed to have lunch and recreation with the other prisoners on remand. While in prison, Jennifer, during our discussions on the state of the organization, would always end her talks with her favorite words, "History will absolve us," referring to Fidel Castro's famous speech made in his defense in court against charges brought against him after he led an attack on the Moncada Barracks in Cuba on October 16, 1953.

This was a time when police and prison officers needed only to be tall, strapping, and able to manhandle prisoners to qualify for the job. It was an old colonial criterion. This was a transitional period as was the case for the wider society; people were now being educated. More educated people formed the prison population, and this new wine was bursting the old wineskins. The prison officers were feeling the ground slipping from under their feet. No longer were they able to use the same old measures to treat this new breed of prisoner.

In the male section of the prison, by this time, there was a large number of NUFF members and others who were sympathetic to the cause. Although left in cells for twenty-three hours, they were instrumental in helping to mobilize the male prisoners who placed mattresses in strategic places and gathered paint and other flammable material. This resulted in a major prison fire, during the aftermath of which, I was told, the corridors were lined with prison officers holding batons. Suspects were made to walk through the aisle created, and they were beaten with batons. Hands and feet were broken; heads were split; and some were more severely punished.

Expectations of being released grew dim. Days turned into weeks, and weeks into months. Daily my hopes were fading as news of guerillas being captured or killed came to my attention. When there was news of guerrillas, they took care to ensure that we neither heard the news nor read the newspapers. All efforts were made to ensure that I was isolated. I had to depend on word of mouth whenever a new prisoner came. The units were being isolated. This seemed to be, without a doubt, the beginning of the end.

Anticipation was building. My trial was about to begin after I had spent about one year in prison on remand. In what appeared to be a very suspicious move, I was suddenly granted bail, a very exorbitant sum. Why now? One week before the trial began, my knight in shining armor came in the person of John Humphrey. One evening while preparing to settle in for the night, I was told to pack my belongings because I was to leave at once; a bailer was at the gate. Was this a trick? With mixed feelings and great misgivings,

I got ready to leave, bidding farewell to my newfound friends and acquaintances.

I later learned that the driver of the black Jaguar that pulled up outside Golden Grove Women's Prison was none other than an advocate of the ideology of Trinityism, of which I had read. He took me to my home. Feeling like a decoy, I visited old friends but stayed away from NUFF. I could not betray the driver's trust in me; I resolved to attend court. He had put his home on the line for mankind since he had posted bail for several of the others.

10

TRIAL AND SENTENCING

My trial began the following week. It was not in my hometown of Point Fortin but in Port of Spain. This was another nightmare. My first thought was to plead guilty and suffer the consequences, but the lawyer felt otherwise. He insisted that we were being tried in a criminal court and would not be allowed to speak of NUFF. Any insistence would be considered contempt of court. I was to place myself far from the scene of the crime. I indicated that I was not comfortable with doing so. He further explained that if I was not guilty of all the counts with which I had been charged, then I had to plead not guilty. There was a trial within a trial to determine the admissibility of my "statement." However, try as I may to explain the circumstances surrounding the alleged statement, it was decided that I had given it voluntarily.

Following are excerpts from the official court record of the cross-examination that took place during the trial. Clinton Whitehead, then the acting superintendent of police attached to CID, Port of Spain, told the court the following:

> I was in my office on the northern side of headquarters, office no. 9, about thirty feet from the open courtyard. Jacob came along with WPC Ewing. There were no other persons when she was brought in. I executed the warrant on her, and I cautioned her.

> I told her, "Do you wish to say anything? You are not obliged to say anything unless you wish to do so. If you say anything, it will be taken down in writing and may be given in evidence."
> She elected to give a statement. I held no promises, I made no threats, I gave no inducements, and I used no force. I wrote the statement myself. I began writing at about three o'clock in the afternoon and finished at nine o'clock at night. I was not writing for six hours. I stopped in between. I was writing and she dictated.

Mr. Lawrence, the lawyer, objected to the admissibility of my statement, saying: "The statement is not voluntary. There were questions and answers, and she was forced to make statements by threats of violence against her person."

The jury was then asked to leave. Whitehead continued:

> I never used force or threats on the accused. A policeman was present throughout. I did not think it necessary that they should sign the statement. A policewoman has to be present when a woman is under arrest. One policeman was present with me throughout the exercise, Inspector Kerr. No other policeman came in. She [meaning me] never protested that she did not wish to sign the statement. Inspector Kerr never asked me for a chance to deal with her.

At this point, Mr. Lawrence questioned whether a policeman who was present there told her [meaning me], "If you do not sign the statement, you will be on your hands and knees begging for mercy."

Mr. Whitehead's response was, "This never happened. ... She [meaning me] was not crying in my office. She came in, sat down, and gave me a statement. It was as simple as that. I never told her that in my twenty-five years as a policeman I had never seen anybody so stubborn, nor did I say that no one who comes to CID leaves without giving a statement. I did not ask her a question; she started to talk, and I wrote .... She never asked Toppin what I was writing. ... I never heard her tell Toppin that she wanted to see a lawyer. I never heard Toppin tell her she was a liar and she could never fool intelligent people. I never heard Toppin tell her he had already sent for her mother and all she had to do was to sign a statement and she would go home .... She never refused to sign.

In her sworn statement, this policewoman police wrote the following:

> My name is Victorine Ewing. I am a woman police constable, 5794, at CID, Port of Spain. On June 25, 1973, I was present at CID. I was with Andrea Jacob guarding her from the morning period until sometime late evening, about seven o'clock. I was at the Narcotics Office at CID with her during the morning period. I can't remember the exact time. I cannot remember how many hours that was. At about a quarter to three in the afternoon, I took her to the superintendent of CID. The office as requested was ASP Whitehead's office. He executed a warrant on her in my presence. He cautioned her, and she said, "I will tell you how I got involved in this thing."
>
> He asked her whether she would like to write down her statement. She replied, "You write it for me."
>
> He then called Inspector Kerr, and we all sat down after she signed the caution and ASP Whitehead recorded a statement from her. This was from about three o'clock in the afternoon to seven o'clock in the evening. I was relieved by WPC Marshall. While I was there, Whitehead did not threaten or hold out any promises to her [meaning me]. No other policeman came into the room while I was there.

ASP Whitehead under cross-examination stated the following:

> I cannot recall whether there was a woman police constable in Toppin's room. There may or may not have been. Toppin asked her questions about a certain organization. Allman did not question her. Toppin did not shout at the accused. I remained for fifteen minutes when I first got there, then I left and made visits to see what was happening.

The policeman who was shouting at me and banging on the table during all this claimed that he had a throat problem that had rendered him incapable of doing these things. I smiled to myself upon realizing that this was obviously the reason he behaved in the manner that he had.

The trial lasted five days, at the end of which I was found guilty of robbery with aggravation and other related charges, including possession of a firearm and kidnapping. I was sentenced to a total of twenty-two years in prison. The lawyer submitted that we members of NUFF were not criminals but revolutionaries.

The judge countered with, "Revolutionaries who miss their mark must be prepared to suffer."

I had been tried along with Clyde Haynes and another person, who were both arrested on the day of the bank robbery and were kept in prison without bail. Charges against the other person were dismissed, while Clyde was sentenced to twelve years in prison.

At age twenty-one, and with the present state of the organization at the time, I saw only doom and gloom. My last words to Clyde, through clenched teeth, were, "Endless jail boy." I ensured that I displayed no emotion.

> I decided to live in the moment and refused to think of what might lie ahead at this point. In the midst of all of this, I was peaceful and calm. I was subsequently escorted to a cell downstairs below the court. It seemed as though the whole of the CID department was taking turns visiting the cell, some hurling harsh remarks,

some showing me pitiful expressions, and others simply wanting to see the "most wanted" prisoner in the flesh. One particular female officer, Majorie Beepathsingh, offered me something to eat or drink. I accepted a carton of juice. Her supervisors, on seeing me with the drink, threatened to dismiss whoever was the culprit, demanding the name of the officer from me. I remained silent. I sat quietly, affirming to myself, "I am spirit; water cannot wet me. Fire cannot burn me. I am one with the oneness of the universe." Later that day, I was taken to Golden Grove Women's Prison.

Andrea Jacob, freedom fighter, after being captured, on her way to court in 1973.

Andrea Jacob on her way to Golden Grove Women's Prison following her trial for bank robbery and other related offenses in 1974.

11

PRISON LIFE

My return to prison as a convicted prisoner was met with silent jubilation on the part of some of the turnkeys. Some of them gloated, while others tried to offer words of encouragement. Within the first few days of my sentence, I made it clear that I wanted no patronizing. I wanted no food from the officers' table or handbags. I would eat what the state provided. Neither was I going to engage in underhanded activities for special favors. I had seen and heard enough of the rottenness of the prison system and therefore was unwilling to be sucked in by it. I was there to serve twenty-two years, although some of the sentences ran concurrently. The lawyer had appealed.

I was angry, emotionally battered, weak, and deflated. I had seen the justice system for what it was, including the lies and fabrications of senior policemen and policewomen whose only interest was in getting a conviction by any means. I was disillusioned because NUFF seemed to be fanning the face of the sun with a feather. I wondered whether death would have been a better fate. I had not counted on this at this crucial stage of my early adulthood, being in the worst place on earth, where I thought I could be for the next nine and a half years at the least. Everything seemed gloomy. The judge's statement about revolutionaries who miss their mark kept playing again and again in my mind.

By now, NUFF was crushed, with polarization having taken

place. Most of the leaders either had been killed or were imprisoned. Members were disillusioned or scared of the extreme violence unleashed by the state. Still others kept a low profile, and some resorted to drug use, maybe to numb the pain.

My mother had been fired from her job as a cook at a shipping company. She still had my younger sister to send to school. While out on bail, I had learned that they were frequently taken from home at very late hours of the night or early morning by the police and dropped off in the middle of nowhere when they failed to give information regarding my whereabouts. They were forced to walk for miles to return home. One day during one of her visits, my mother said to me, "Don't be surprised if you hear that I'm in the square with my bundle on my head." I knew exactly what this meant. She was alluding to a place where the homeless, the insane, and other vagrants were found. I felt her pain.

One of the brothers from the unit in Point Fortin was followed and severely beaten after visiting me at the prison. I had no intention of placing further burdens on my family to secure legal fees, having already abandoned my role as breadwinner, and therefore, amid many ambivalent thoughts and without consulting with the lawyer or anyone, I withdrew my appeal. After all, I had helped to liberate the funds from the bank.

Following the withdrawal of the appeal, I withdrew from everyone. I stopped sending out all visit forms because I felt that visitation was the system's way of monitoring what was taking place in my mind. I stopped writing letters and only spoke when necessary. The sentence seemed like an eternity. There seemed to be no end to this tunnel.

I was now a convicted prisoner. I had to store my clothes and other personal belongings and change into prison gear. I took up residence in the dormitory alongside the other convicts. I was given the most menial tasks to perform, such as stooping or bending over in a concrete drain that passed through the premises and scrubbing the moss that had accumulated there and in the yard with large yard brooms and steel brushes, also cleaning the prisoners' toilets and bathroom, which was tedious, monotonous, unproductive, and boring. The concrete was always wet and cold, and I would experience severe back and abdominal pains and cramps, especially when menstruating. I refused to complain, fully understanding my taskmasters' objectives. When I was joined by a sister of a deceased NUFF brother, our rallying cry was "Night must come." We neither disobeyed instructions nor stopped working, but we did work as slow as was humanly possible in one spot. We utilized our personal shampoo and bath soaps to ensure that the prisoners' toilet and bathroom were immaculately clean.

I was now a regular visitor to the cellblock where I spent considerable time in solitary confinement. It was now my sanctuary, my place of refuge. I had to find the mental strength to survive in this place. With the dehumanization, contamination, loss of identity, and turning of prisoners into nonpersons, the monotony of the place was proving too much for me to bear. I felt as though I were sinking in quicksand.

The loneliness of prison life was beyond description. It was agonizing and painful. At times I would be happy to see an ant in my cell. I would speak to it and follow it around for hours, ensuring that it did not leave. I looked forward to the ray of sun that would come through the tiny vent in the cellblock, and I would position myself so that it made contact with my hands or feet. I discovered that the hairs on my body reflected the colors of the rainbow when exposed to the sun's rays at a particular time of the day. Once, when a tiny kitten strayed into the cell, I ensured that it was fed so that it would come by every evening. We developed a great friendship until it stopped visiting or was prevented from doing so.

I thought a great deal about my family, feeling that only my mother and younger sister understood. The others were either ashamed because of what some people would think, were afraid of the police, or were sorry for me. And then my students. I wondered how the sudden turn of events had impacted their young minds.

Over the last couple of years before my absence, I had undergone a lot of changes and mental conditioning as an urban guerrilla, facilitated by the literature I read and the hardship I experienced. However, to my neighbors and friends, I still was the innocent little country girl who had grown up before their very eyes. Some people even speculated that I had either been drugged or brainwashed, I was told. I knew, however, that this was all part of the price that I had to pay for the path that I and the others had embarked upon.

My thoughts of Johnny and others who had "tripped," or died, were that they had gone on to another dimension. I knew that they would have chosen death over imprisonment, so I did not worry too much about them. My concern was, what was my destiny? I felt that this being imprisoned was a fate worse than death.

There were times when I was so overwhelmed by my then current situation that I just wanted to cry myself to sleep, but try as I might, the tears just failed to come. My tear ducts just refused to cooperate. The former I believe, would have been less painful than the latter.

The isolation, the pain of confinement, to which I was not accustomed, became excruciating. I felt that I would lose my mind. I was descending into this dark hole from which I could see no way out. I severed communication with everyone and withdrew into myself.

I was determined to prove that my spirit could not and would not be broken by the corrupt capitalist system, whereas I think the officers had opposing thoughts. One insisted that the prison was an arm of the police. If we wanted to fight and kill police, and being that the police were their brothers, then I should not expect to "make an easy jail." In light of this, I strategized that first I would prove that I had no fear of solitary confinement. This I did by refusing to obey orders that were given in a derogatory manner. I would say to the jailer, "I am not doing it. Put me in the cell" or "Lock me up," or just remain silent. They could not understand and were baffled by the fact that big strong men were usually afraid of confinement and punishment and would come out of the cellblock weakened, dreading to face the light and fearful of returning, whereas I did not seem to care. When exiting, if challenged, I was prepared to reenter.

I had my Bible and a picture of a lighted candle, which I sometimes used to meditate, and I would do my yoga exercises.

In prison, one could be charged for anything once one failed to cooperate with the system. One could be charged for insolence if one said what was really on one's mind, or dumb insolence if one remained silent. The turnkeys and orderlies provoked us prisoners, using our fear of losing remission to keep us in line. The system was not designed for prisoners to come out on top.

Another fear that I had to overcome was the fear of hunger, so as soon as I was placed in the cell, I stopped eating. One would be punished by being given a restricted diet consisting of bread and water, or bread and flour porridge sweetened with salt instead of sugar and milk; or for long periods, flour dumplings and potatoes. This was usually for seven, fourteen, or twenty-one days. One was first subjected to an examination by the doctor to determine whether or not one was fit for this form of punishment.

The third fear that I had to overcome was of not having my time curtailed. Prisoners generally would do anything to leave prison at the earliest possible time since with "good behavior" a prison year for female prisoners could be shortened to eight months. I would challenge the turnkeys to take my days.

When placed on punishment in the cell, one's bed is removed and replaced with a wooden plank about eight feet by four feet. One is given a potty and an enamel jug of water. I would drink a few sips of water occasionally, and do my yoga exercises, which included deep breathing while sitting cross-legged or shallow breathing while lying in the Death Pose, which I mainly did to conserve energy. At times the turnkeys and orderlies had to call or enter the cell to determine whether I was still on this physical plane of existence. They theorized that I practiced high science and disappeared, and therefore had to be watched around the clock. The police had found yoga books during some of their raids on places occupied by the guerrillas—hence their assumption. Most of the time mankind had eluded them.

A teacher who seemed to be in her eighties would come to

the prison to give classes on the three R's: reading, writing, and arithmetic. One day I decided to attend the class out of boredom.

The teacher cunningly mentioned something about the police killing of Guy Harewood, and then she said, "Speak the truth and speak it ever." I looked up at her, and she looked at me. In that brief moment, I felt as if she had gotten a glimpse of my soul. This was one of the most profound lessons I think she had ever taught. It was just her penmanship text for that day. To me, it was confirmation that I should have followed my inner convictions and pled guilty as charged even though I was unable to state the reason for my actions. I reminded myself that the lawyer had said that I could not do this because I was not guilty of all the counts. Since it felt like a confusing no-win situation, I just vowed to speak the truth regardless of the consequences.

Letters and greeting cards were coming from around the world from people in solidarity with our struggle. There were those from Amnesty International, *The Rebel*, *Race Today*, and *Caribbean Digest*, and from Holland, England, and other parts of the world. There were also some that were local. I would be notified of their arrival by orderlies, but most of them never reached me. They were censored. There were three, however, that were of great significance to me.

One of the most touching and most memorable letters I received came from a then nine-year-old student who wrote expressing how much she loved me and missed me. It reads in part:

> We shall not be great friends. We shall be the *greatest of all friends*. This I know. I am still praying for you, and I know everything will be all right. Bye for now.
>
> With a lot of love,
Suzette

There was also a very shocking one. It came from my prior form mistress who likened our struggle to that engaged in by Maurice Bishop of Grenada and other freedom fighters around the world. She seemed to have understood it all. There was, however, this strange letter with symbolic drawings stating that it was my case against God, urging me to fight and assuring me that I would win. It was signed by El Millionario Negro. I had no idea who the writer was, but that letter was a tremendous inspiration to me at the time I received it. It served as a lifeline. I knew then that I had to continue the fight by employing different strategies. I had to go on.

> "We shall not be great friends, we shall be the "GREATEST OF ALL FRIENDS", this I know.
>
> I am still praying for you and know everything will be alright. Bye for now.
>
> With lot of Love
> Suzette"

Excerpt from a letter written by a former student, 1974.

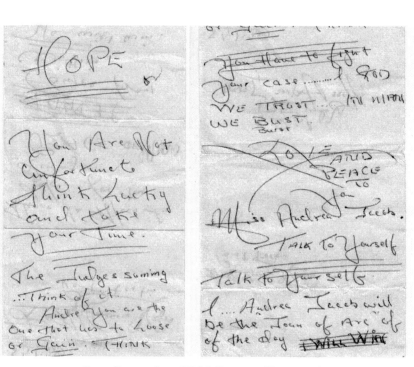

Above: Letter from El Millionario Negro, 1974.

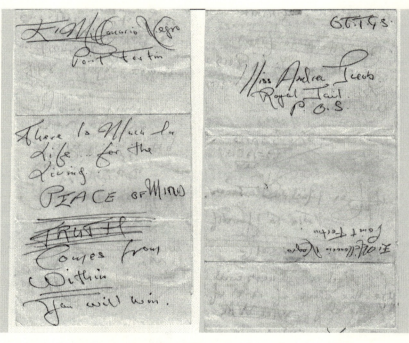

Above: Letter from El Millionario Negro (cont'd), 1974.

During my time spent on the cellblock, I read the Bible from cover to cover, not understanding most of what I read. However, the more I studied the Word, the more I became convicted of the sin in my life. I began to realize how far I had strayed from the way that Christ taught. It was as if I were in a quagmire from which I could not escape. I needed salvation. My life, mind, and sanity depended upon it. I repented of my sins, at which time a deep sense of remorse came over me and I surrendered to God.

Around this same time, I dreamt that I was going through a cemetery and that huge fireballs were falling from the sky and crashing all around me. I began to run, but they were falling from every direction. I was trapped. One fell near me, and I fell to the ground. It was then that I saw my life flash before my eyes in a split second, and then it started rebuilding. Like a jigsaw puzzle, the parts of my life began fitting together, giving meaning to things I had not previously understood. I woke up and remembered Johnny's experience, which he had described to me, about that night when the police dog had come upon him. It was a similar experience where his life had flashed before his eyes in a split second. It was only then that I think I fully understood what he had meant. I began reading my Bible like never before.

The Word became like oxygen to me. I needed it to survive. What was happening to me? I couldn't understand. As if by compulsion, I had to read the Word. It was as though I would die if I didn't read it. I would have a little New Testament in my bosom, and at every opportunity I got, I would go to the washroom and read. I would read at the lunch table and after work was over. I would ask to go to the dormitory so that I could read. I would read and read. It was as though my life, my sanity, depended on it, as if I would lose my mind if I didn't read the Word. My mind was being reorganized, almost as if it was being re-formed by the Word of God. Revelations were now bursting into my consciousness. With scriptures that I had learned, read, or heard in the past, the meanings were being revealed and were being applied to my life.

I began to cry out to God, "Why? Why is this happening? Am I losing my mind? Why have so many people been killed? Imprisoned? My family members, why do they have to suffer? Why did you allow us to go on thinking that you were with us, that we were doing your will? Is there a God? If so, then reveal yourself to me!" I was desperate.

On that particular night, I cried myself to sleep. I had another dream. In this one, I received a long letter with my name, Andrea, the meaning of which has to do with beginnings and endings. Lucina, my other name, originates from the Latin word for light. I was born the first day of the last month, the alpha and the omega. Then I was told, "We know all that is happening with you, but we could not reveal ourselves to you until now." It was a long letter. I woke up with a peace like that described in the Holy Bible, "the peace that passes understanding."

In the weeks that followed, I felt nothing but love for everyone. Nothing anyone did or said offended me. It was as though my mind was caught up in another dimension. Initially, I had found great solace in songs such as Bob Marley's "War" and Calypsonian Gypsy's "I Am a Warrior," and other songs of rebellion. I now found myself gravitating toward more spiritual songs. Among my favorites were "By the Waters of Babylon," "Hear, O Lord," and "Man Is Lonely by Birth."

Even the prison officers noticed the change that came over me. They began to say to prisoners, the new arrivals, "You are here for seven days [or one month], and you are crying as though it's the end of the world. Look at Andrea Jacob: she behaves as though she is just here for a day."

It was during this time that I came across a prayer entitled "A Freeman's Prayer" by James Dillet Freeman, which became my mantra. Some of the words with which I identified are as follows:

> To you, I entrust my life, my country, and my ideals.
> I work not to destroy, but to preserve the good.
> The victory for which I work, for which I try to serve,
> Is the victory of all humanity.

> Lord, lead me on to the tasks which lie ahead of me,
> To the labors of uniting the nations of the earth,
> To the peace founded not on force but on mutual respect
> of all free men.

One day I distinctly heard a voice saying to me, "The Word is spirit and life. You all wanted to give the people material things such as food, clothes, and houses, but with the same spirit in a man, he would abuse them all. I am taking you to another level, the spiritual, where the work is." I did not fully understand these things, but I had a thirst for a deeper understanding of God. Nothing else mattered.

12

CONVERSION

My trips to the cellblock, which consisted of three separate cells where prisoners were isolated as a form of punishment for wrongdoings, became even more frequent. I sometimes provoked the turnkeys and orderlies into punishing me by refusing to obey their instructions. The cellblock became my oasis.

I increasingly felt that I needed to be alone to find the God whom I was so desperately seeking or who was seeking me. I had so many questions for which I needed answers, and I believed that only he could supply them. The holy books and doctrines of the various religions, including the Koran of the Muslims and the Bhagavad Gita of the Hindus; the works of Ellen G. White of the Seventh-day Adventists, Tuesday Lobsang Rampa of Zen Buddhism, the Unity school of Christianity, and Charles Taze Russell of the Jehovah's Witnesses; and different versions of the Bible were among the literature I explored. I was comparing them to one another, seeking the ways they were similar and the ways they were different.

All religions made the claim of having a direct line to God. Which one was the truth? Were there basic principles common to all religions? If so, what were they? Are the different religions different paths all leading to the same ocean? The Bible says that no one can come to the Father except through Jesus Christ the Son, that he is the way and the door. However, if a person is born in another religion and carries out all the dictates of his religion or his tribe but never hears of Jesus, what is his lot when he dies? Does God have a mother? I had to know these things.

I was ready to surrender. I began to engage in deep soul-searching. Previously, I had adopted other people's ideologies. What was mine? I was familiar with the saying "Man, know thyself," but who was I? I still needed answers.

I was a vegetarian, and there were turnkeys and prison orderlies who would ensure that meat sauce and meat were all over my food, forcing me not to eat. I felt that I was wasting my life and saw the insane asylum as my possible next stop. I also experienced severe back pain. Based on all this, it was "do or die." Something had to give. I decided to go on a hunger strike. What was the point of living? I stopped eating or accepting meals. I only got out of my bed to bathe, exercise, and occasionally have a few sips of water. I went down to 94 pounds from approximately 118 pounds.

In that seclusion, I thought long and hard. Was this the way I wanted to go? Where could I go from here? I read the letter from El Millionario Negro over and over. I thought about all the beautiful people who had risked their lives or given their lives or in some other way had supported the cause, including those who had been expressing their love and solidarity and also contributed in both tangible and intangible ways.

I kept on praying, seeking divine direction, and came up with a vision and goal to further my studies, thereby making myself more self-reliant should I survive imprisonment.

The commissioner of prisons then came to visit me in my cell. I refused to stand, as was the rule when visited by senior officers, or get up from my bed. He tried to coax me to do so, claiming that he wanted to help me but saying he could not if I did not speak to him. I finally gestured for him to get me a pen and paper, on which I wrote my requests for a vegetarian diet and to be allowed to pursue academic studies. I promised to speak with a doctor, following which my requests were granted. I was placed on light labor because of my medical problems and was allowed to begin a course of study. I needed mentally stimulating books.

I was teased by the then adviser to the commissioner of prisons, Mr. Desmond Cartey, who expressed that I could not study in that environment. I took up the challenge, and he made me a bet that I could not pass three subjects at GCE. Should I pass three subjects, he offered to make me a promise that he was not willing to disclose at the time. Some turnkeys were not so generous once I began to study. They would turn up the radio, which they would normally have off, and use it to punish the prisoners. They employed their divide-and-rule policy by inciting the prisoners against me, claiming that I wanted to deprive them of their rights by wanting the volume turned down so that I could study. Among the remarks made was that I was a prisoner like everyone else and therefore did not deserve special treatment. Someone said that if I wanted to study, I should have stayed out of prison. However, I felt that I owed it to the others to succeed since by doing so I would be making a way for them. I also had aspirations to meet the university entry requirements.

The commissioner of prisons at that time was Tom Isles. During his visits to the women's prison, he would often, to the officers' chagrin, call me and ask for a chair to be brought for me to sit, which was unheard of at the women's prison. Prisoners sitting on the same chairs as officers! After he left, they would have the other prisoners scrub and disinfect the chair.

During these times, I would be allowed to engage Tom Isles in discourses on topics such as the prison conditions, the society we live in, and my reason for taking the road we of NUFF took, which I believe intrigued him since he always sought an audience with me. I would talk about the inadequacy of the available reading material in the prison; the need for a proper library, continuing education, and skills training for prisoners; and the lack of properly trained prison officers, who I felt had only gotten the job because they were robust and able to manhandle prisoners, the emphasis being more on brawn than on brains.

I expressed that a new breed of more intelligent prisoners was now entering the penal system, necessitating a stepping up of the training of prison officers to meet their needs. This training should include courses in psychology and communication, I said. I likened the present system to dogs being placed in a cage and being stuck by *cocoyea* sticks and punished when they barked or bit in retaliation. Convicts were coming into the prison with their myriad social problems, and because of the inadequacy of the officers, they were battered, provoked, cussed at, and derided instead of being understood, supported, and encouraged to change.

My stay in prison was tumultuous at times with frequent trips to the office for trial for offenses such as using obscene language and assaulting an officer, which I usually did in self-defense after they committed some offense against me. There were times of relative calm. Going to the front yard to enjoy the trees, the flowers, the birds, and other aspects of nature was a special treat carried out by the braver officers. On one such occasion, I used green tea plants and wrote "Golden Grove Women's Prison" in a large arc toward the front of the building. The commissioner was impressed by this and consented that I be allowed in the garden regularly. This had its other advantages. I was able to see and get a quick wave to the male prisoners or send a message to the brothers who were doing time, among other things, as they passed in their work gangs, depending on which officer was on duty.

While in prison, I was learning other aspects of life in the city and about Mastifay, Jean in Town, Dr. Rat, Al Capone, and the different unique and interesting characters seemingly known by all in the ghettos in the city. I heard about the music and clashes of Desperadoes Steel Orchestra, Casablanca, and Red Army, among others; learned of the activities that were engaged in at the Gateway, Club 101, and the Miramar; and heard stories of murder, robbery, gambling, and prostitution. I was getting a glimpse of the real world, as few people from the part of the society I came from ever went to prison.

Even in the prison, one could see the hierarchic structure of the wider plantation society. There were the senior officers, the junior officers, and orderlies of various ranks, or "house niggers," and then there were the "lumpen" prisoners who can be compared to the field slaves.

My participation in a basic and advanced sewing course where I came out as top of the class led to my being made supervisor of the sewing class that made clothes and linens for the female prisoners. I was also responsible for distributing linen and clothing to new prisoners upon their arrival. This was not compulsory. It was my choice.

While reading a Daily Blessing booklet, I came across the phrase "Bloom where you are planted." This hit me like a bolt of lightning. I began to meditate on those words and began conversing with myself: *Why do I feel like I should not be in here? Who said that I was to be teaching at Fanny Village Government School?* I concluded that this was just the place I needed to be since God's people were here and there were lessons to be learned here as well as lessons to be taught.

This was my wake-up call. I began seeking out opportunities to be of service to others. I counseled and advised prisoners about their various social issues. I lived on a subsistence minimum, sharing my soap, shampoo, toothpaste, and other toiletries with prisoners who did not have them. I had my Seventh-day Adventist sister "Lel," along with her network, come visit and encourage families of prisoners on the outside, also assisting them with necessities. I assisted by writing letters, especially for the prohibited immigrants from Spanish-speaking countries who were usually arrested at nightclubs and hotels for soliciting passengers. They were usually from Colombia, Venezuela, or Santo Domingo. I was happy for the opportunity to practice the Spanish language, which I had learned at school, acting as an interpreter at times.

Sometime in 1979, there was a pregnant prisoner for whom I was instrumental in having Lel take her baby from the hospital following his birth and raise him until she was released from prison. This goodwill was extended to officers too as I took up their cases and stood up for them, especially young recruits when I felt they were being oppressed or victimized by their seniors—and especially those who tried to be humane to me. A senior officer once asked, "Who does Andrea Jacob think she is, Mr. Thomasos?" She was referring to the then Speaker of the House of Representatives.

The dreams continued. In one of them, I saw a Bible in the sky with its pages opened to Psalm 20. I was still seeking to understand whether people of the different ethnic groups should remain with their traditional religions. There was so much being said about the white man and his imposing his religion on the slaves to keep them in subjection. In Trinidad and Tobago, a law was passed forbidding Spiritual Baptists from practicing their faith. I thought then that this must truly be the black person's religion. However, in another dream, I saw Jesus as a little white boy on the beach, then as a black boy in an African rainforest, and the revelation broke that Jesus is all things to all human beings.

I remember that some time before the bank robbery, I had seen Johnny with a thin leather string with a pouch attached to it around his neck. I asked him what it signified, and he replied that a brother had given it to him, telling him that once he wore it, he would not be killed. I inquired if he believed that to be true, and his response was, "Well, so far, so good."

I was curious to find out the contents of the pouch and sought Johnny's permission to open it, which he granted. Opening the pouch, I found a piece of parchment paper, on which was written, "He that dwelleth in the secret place of the Most High shall abide under the shadow of the Almighty," a verse from Psalm 91, taken from the Bible. I had often thought of the fact that I had opened the pouch and that Johnny was killed soon after, while I was now in prison, but I reasoned that his time had come to go and someone had to release him from the guard. Maybe I was that person. Quite a few other brothers and sisters had sought baptism mainly by Spiritual Baptists, but all were seeking God's guidance and protection.

One day, I was suddenly told to stop work, bathe, and change, following which I was escorted to the front gallery, where visits were received. To my pleasant surprise, there sat my mother. Mere words cannot describe the feelings and emotions that engulfed me. I smiled broadly and can only say euphemistically that I was happy to see her.

The commissioner of prisons had arranged for the welfare officer to visit her and facilitate this visit. I resumed writing letters and sending visit forms at this point. However, I was still cautious about writing to NUFF members or others who could be incriminated.

My quest continued, as did the dreams. I had this one dream where I was at Fanny Village, my hometown, walking along the beach. When I entered the water, which was rough and dirty, it suddenly became calm and crystal clear. My friend, who was walking along the shore, expressed her surprise that the water had become clean when I entered it. My response was, "I'm pure." Suddenly I saw what looked like a temple coming toward the shore. A figure like Jesus was standing at the front with an open book in his hand the size of a pocket-sized New Testament.

I went out of the water while the temple floated toward the shore. I had climbed up the bank onto the hill, upon which different religious leaders began assembling. There were about thirty of them running to and fro, trying to follow from their blue books, which they had in their hands, but they all had the wrong books. Eventually, they came to me to borrow my book, which I had in my pocket. Jesus read; they followed. Then they returned the book to me. The page from which Jesus had read was numbered 118. I told them it belonged to me and, therefore, that I would read it later, then continued changing my clothes. The full significance of this dream, I could not possibly grasp at that time. However, I regularly read Psalm 118.

This was followed by another dream. In this one, I was in a little room with a Baptist leader dressed in a brown gown with a shepherd's rod in his hand. He was someone with whom I was familiar since in the past I had witnessed many baptisms he had performed in the name of the Father, the Son, and the Holy Ghost. In the dream, I had gone to him to be baptized. There was carpet on the floor. When I lifted the carpet, there was board. I kept lifting layers of carpet and board but could not find the earth, which I was seeking. Two years later, I had an identical dream, but this time I was taken to an upper room where there was a large book, which I was told was the book of life. I identified my name therein and was led into another room, this one was filled with books.

The significance of all this was not revealed to me until many years later. However, at the time it served to strengthen my belief in a higher power and in the idea that such a power was leading and guiding me.

Meanwhile, I wrote and passed three GCE O-level subjects and also studied and passed English Literature at the advanced level, along with pursuing studies in economics and sociology. I just wanted to get all the reading material that I could lay my hands on. When the new commissioner of prisons, Mr. Randolph Charles, realized that I had passed mathematics on my first attempt, he told me that I had shown potential, so in the future, they would sponsor all my exams. Before it was Roman Catholic archbishop Anthony Pantin and the abbot at Mount Saint Benedict, Abbot Hildebrandt Greene, who had been providing financial and other support.

13

NUFF SPEAKS FROM PRISON

One day I received an astonishing letter from Terrence "Tuku" Thornhill, the brother with whom I had entered the bank arm in arm as part of our disguise as a couple. He had abandoned his studies at a university abroad and, accompanied by a friend, was traveling on a motorbike to the Himalayas in search of spiritual enlightenment. His ambition was to "find the truth and be able to share it with at least one person." This journey had to be aborted when war broke out in Bangladesh, at which time he decided to return to Trinidad. On his return to the country in 1971, he found his best friend Guy Harewood involved in the revolution. This resulted in his subsequently becoming a part of NUFF.

His letter reads in part:

> Our loving Lord Jesus has come into my life and has changed it all around I serve him now with all my heart, and I am no longer involved in politics. He has shown me, by Revelation, that that is not the way. He is the only way. For sons and daughters of God are heaven-bound creatures, pilgrims sojourning in this strange land for a short time.
>
> The enemy is not flesh and blood, but the devil and all his copartners, colleagues, spirits instruments, et al., and he comes at us through all different forms. Man is given power less than an angel, and Satan is an archangel

and has a team of fallen angels for whom we are no match. Christ Jesus our Lord and Savior is the only one who has overcome Satan, and it is only him in us that can overcome the evil in this world.

    Sister Andrea, I pray that the Lord Jesus reveals himself to you and fills you with his love, peace, and joy. May the Lord God bless and keep you.

Brother Terry

I was stunned, to say the least. Tuku had gone through a spiritual conversion at about the same time that a spiritual change was taking place in me, which as yet I did not fully understand.

Our Loving Lord Jesus has come into my life and has changed it all around. I serve Him now with all my heart and I am no longer involved in politics. He has shown me, by Revelation, that that is not the way. He is the only way, for sons and daughters of God are heaven-bound creatures, — pilgrims sojourning in this strange land for a short time. The enemy is not flesh and blood, but the Devil and all his co-partners, colleagues, spirits, instruments, etc, and he comes at us thru all different forms. Man is given power less than an angel and Satan is an arch-angel and has a team of fallen angels for whom we are no match. Christ Jesus our Lord and Saviour is the only one that has overcome satan, and it's only Him in us can overcome the evil in this world. Sister Andrea I pray that the Lord Jesus reveals Himself to you and fills you with His love, peace and joy. Amen.

Him. Hoping to hear from you soon sister. May the Lord God bless and keep you. Amen.

Brother Terry.

Excerpt from a letter written by Terrance Thornhill in 1975.

While still in prison, I also learned that there was disagreement between those brothers with religious persuasions and those with a hard-line Marxist ideology.

Simultaneously, the brothers in prison had been having heated discussions on religion vs. revolution. Some, of the view that religion was antiscientific, embraced technology and every achievement that the natural sciences had made, while not wanting social science to reach the masses for fear that it would be used as a tool against the ruling class. They cited revolutionary thinkers such as Mao, Cabral, Lenin, and Castro, among others, as having all used science to liberate the oppressed people of their respective countries while questioning what religion has done for the oppressed peoples of the world. They also put forward the view that religious leaders joined with the ruling class of exploiters to take away the fruits of the labor of the masses of people.

On the other hand, others felt that religion established guidelines by which humankind must be governed or to which humankind must submit, which they saw as the thing able to bring about moral and revolutionary discipline. They had produced a booklet entitled *NUFF Speaks from Prison* in which their opposing views were expressed. It was made up of letters from both outside and inside prison outlining the different arguments and also stating the plight of those incarcerated. At the same time this discourse was being engaged in, I was being called out of religion and unto Christ, the Word of God.

Andrea Jacob attending court, 1974.

Clyde Haynes, jointly charged with Andrea Jacob, 1974.

Terrence Thornhill following his release from prison in 1975.

Andrea's graduation from the University of the West Indies–Saint Augustine, Trinidad, 2005.

14

POSTPRISON

In early 1981, when it was time for me to leave prison, I had no feelings of hostility, animosity, or hatred toward anyone either inside the prison or on the outside. After my departure, I sent back thank-you cards to the prison officers and also to some of the prisoners, to whom I wrote and some of whose families I visited on their behalf. I also visited my old teacher colleagues as well as the principal. Most of the pupils had moved on to secondary school or higher education, while others had families of their own.

Life as I knew it had changed considerably. My visits to past members of NUFF revealed that some had been so traumatized by the events of the past years that they had just channeled their energy into caring for their families, doing their jobs, or pursuing the arts. Others went on to higher education, while still others, out of absolute frustration, went on to abuse drugs, mainly marijuana or cocaine.

Ten days after leaving prison, I paid a visit to Mr. Desmond Cartey, the former adviser to the commissioner of prisons, who was then minister of labor. He kept the promise he had made to me during my incarceration. By three o'clock in the afternoon of that very day, I was employed, performing clerical duties. I was assured that I would not be fired, but there was no avenue for upward mobility.

The country had changed noticeably. The economy was not as depressed as before, and Trinidad and Tobago had experienced an oil boom. At Point Fortin, most of the youths were now gainfully employed in the oil industry. Even the cultural changes that had previously taken place had regressed. The militant atmosphere that had prevailed in the country during the late 1960s and early 1970s no longer existed. I wondered whether the society had become so traumatized that it had gone into shock after the events of the 1970s or if people no longer cared and were quite content to "join them since they couldn't beat them."

Most of the black consciousness that had been generated had fizzled out. Sisters went back to straightening their hair and using other chemicals on it. Dashiki and other forms of African wear were no longer as prevalent as before.

Even the Rastafarian movement, which had taken Trinidad and Tobago by storm, was not as vibrant as before. The sisters were no longer dressing the part by wearing their long skirts and natural hairstyles, either having cut their dreadlocks or now wearing them in a stylish way. Even the Bush People, Mother Earth, and many others who had rejected the "Babylonian system," opting to leave their homes and live in the forest, dressing in crocus bags or wearing no clothes at all, were no longer heard of. Most had abandoned their communes and returned to civilization.

Most of the members of NUFF who had not been murdered were out of prison, having won their cases. Some were out on bail with cases pending; some had been pardoned; and a few were still doing time. I was elated to see the ones who were out of prison, but I felt a sense of deep dejection for those who were still locked up or had been severely traumatized by it all.

I continued to find strength and solace in songs. Jimmy Cliff's "Born to Win" emerged as my anthem. I particularly identified with the lines, "I was born to win. I am a Daniel in the lions' den, Jonah in the belly of the whale. I am not alone, so I cannot fail, no, no, no. I am born to win." Among my other favorites were Bob Marley's "Redemption Song" and Calypsonian Valentino's "Life Is a Stage." There were others.

After about two years of being plagued by the feeling that I was wasting what was left of my life, I wrote to the prime minister at the time, Mr. George Chambers, informing him that I wanted to pursue a degree in social work. By October 1983, I was granted a scholarship and began my studies at the University of the West Indies in Mona, Jamaica. However, I first had to be interviewed by Mr. Randolph Burroughs, who by then had been promoted to commissioner of police. Expressing that he was happy to see me, he, as was his usual modus operandi, was apologetic for my demise. He congratulated me for seeking higher education despite all that I had been through. Our discourse ended with his asking for an honest answer to a question he posed.

"Jay, tell me, if you had the chance to live your life all over, do you think that you would do the same things that you did?"

I replied, "I firmly believe that conditions create the basis for action and are equal to it. However, the same conditions do not present themselves at any other time in one's life." He looked at me as though soaking in the gravity of what I had said, then smiled.

Mr. Burroughs was head of the Flying Squad, which was a special police unit formed in 1970 after the Black Power uprisings, whose main target became the National United Freedom Fighters. He had handpicked all the men in his Flying Squad, and they were answerable only to him since at the time there was no oversight body to question the actions of the police. The Flying Squad became famous for their relentless pursuit of NUFF, killing more than eighteen of its members, but they fell from grace when the Scotts Drug Report, authored by the Commission of Inquiry into the Extent of the Problem of Drug Abuse in Trinidad and Tobago, produced "evidence of engagement by policemen in criminal acts including smuggling, counterfeiting, and probably murder." Randolph Burroughs left office in disgrace after being sacked and charged with conspiracy to commit murder.

While in Jamaica, I learned of the murder of Maurice Bishop, for whom I had tremendous admiration. He was a brilliant and courageous revolutionary who gave his life for the liberation and advancement of the Grenadian and Caribbean masses. He was the founder of the New Jewel Movement and the People's Revolutionary Government of Grenada, which staged a revolution in that country in March of 1979, deposing the Grenada United Labor Party, which was led by Eric Gairy, and setting the country on a new socioeconomic and political path. This was described by Fidel Castro, the president of Cuba at the time, as "a big revolution in a small country."

Bishop's refusal to share power with his deputy led to his being deposed and placed under house arrest. On October 19, 1983, he was executed by firing squad along with several other members of his cabinet. It was a difficult period for me: this occurrence served to open old wounds, as Grenada's revolution embodied most of the philosophical ideologies of the NUFF movement and was seen as a great success within the Caribbean region. I cried upon receiving the news. The atmosphere on the campus was somber in most quarters.

I had gotten married before leaving for Jamaica, so my stay there was challenging in many ways. I worked hard at my studies, keeping on my desk a card that I had purchased at a bookstore that read, "THERE IS NO SUCH THING AS CAN'T." I graduated with honors.

On my return to Trinidad, I began work in the community of Fanny Village, becoming the manager of a sports and cultural club, Coconut United. To help with literacy issues among the people, I went on a book drive, soliciting new and used books from individuals in the community, the library at Point Fortin, and bookstores as far as San Fernando.

A makeshift library was constructed downstairs in my home, where activities such as spelling bees, storytelling, and reading competitions were engaged in. Books were borrowed by both adults and children, and tokens were given as incentives. Since the nearest library was approximately three miles away, these activities were welcomed by all.

All manner of sports were engaged in, including night cricket, basketball, netball, tennis, and all fours. I had learned to play badminton in Jamaica, and very soon, everyone was playing it on the street. The mayor happened to pass one evening. On seeing the large group gathered in the fading light in the street in front of my home playing, he was so impressed that within a month we had streetlights beneath which to play.

Competitions and cultural exchanges were undertaken with other groups and villages as far as Le Platte Village, our sister group. These usually ended with a beach lime (hangout). We hosted ice cream parties for the youths, and tea parties and fashion shows for the elderly. A caroling group was formed to take the good tidings of the birth of Jesus Christ to the community around Christmastime. Educational outings to the Pitch Lake at La Brea, the beach at Vessigny, and the Mall at Gulf City were arranged for the children who at that time did not have the resources to benefit from those activities. We staged midnight Olympics, ten-cent concerts, cookouts, and other activities, uniting and spreading love in the community, all of which went on for a while until I changed residence.

Above: Andrea's children, Carlan and Denzyl, 1991.
Left: Andrea at home with her sons in 1994.
Right: Andrea with family, 1995.

Son's graduation, 2002.

I gained employment for a short while as a youth officer and later as a social worker and subsequently became the mother of two boys. My search for meaning in my life was not over; I still had that void within. The scripture "Unless a man is born of water and the Holy Spirit, he cannot enter the kingdom of heaven" kept coming back to my remembrance. I began attending different denominational churches in search of the right one, knowing that I wanted to serve God in spirit and truth, but still being uncertain as to where my calling was. I kept praying, asking for divine direction.

One day I saw on television a local Pentecostal pastor who spoke of miracles and healings. I went to him, told him my story, and asked to be baptized. A couple of days later, I was baptized by him. He advised that for purposes of convenience, I could attend at the nearest Full Gospel church, since his church was a great distance from where I lived. I soon found a nearby church that I began attending. I knew from reading the Bible that I should stop partying, partaking in alcohol, and getting involved with other things in the world. Yet, somehow, I felt that I was not changed. Gradually I began to gravitate to my former ways.

Sometime after this, I visited a privately owned home for the aged as part of my duties as a social worker. The owner of the home was out of sight, so I spoke to the receptionist. As she left the room to inform the owner of my presence, I took a quick look around the premises.

On entering the room, the owner burst into speaking in an unknown tongue or language. She was a mother of a Spiritual Baptist church. At first, I thought that she was angry because of my actions. I asked her the meaning of her utterances, to which she responded with a question: "Which church do you attend?" After I answered her, she began again to speak in the unknown language and then interpreted what she had said: "You do not belong there."

I asked her, "Where do I belong?"

She responded, "You belong to the Order of Melchizedek."

"What is that?"

"The order to which Jesus belonged." Each time she spoke, she said what she wanted in the other language, then interpreted it. This conversation continued for a while, then we proceeded to dealing with the business for which I had come. I was a bit perplexed by the strange events of that day. I had many questions. That night I pondered on all that the woman had said and decided to seek further clarification.

In the days that followed, we engaged in lengthy discussions on the Word and our beliefs. I had questions: Why do you light candles to pray when the Bible states that Jesus is the light of the world? Why the ringing of the bell, tying of the head, and other rituals?

Sometime after, I visited the mother of the NUFF sisters from Crystal Stream. I had enquired about Jinx, a then sixteen-year-old boy whom I had met for the first time at the house at Village Council Street. He used to be very helpful to the brothers but had subsequently been sentenced to life in prison for murder and other charges. She informed me of his release from prison and the fact that he was now married, had given his life to Christ, and was now attending services at the church named Yad-El Tabernacle pastored by Brother Terrance Thornhill.

Brother Terry, as he was now called, had had his twenty-five charges against him dismissed after appealing to the Privy Council on grounds that his constitutional rights had been infringed when he was denied the right to have his lawyer present while giving statements to the police on all his charges at the time of his arrest. This case is considered a landmark civil rights case and one that is compulsory to know when studying law in the Caribbean.

I had attended a few services at Terry's church, where he had preached in the past. What caught my attention was the fact that the women did not wear pants, instead wearing very long skirts, and wore no other jewelry besides their wedding or engagement rings. They had no makeup on their faces, and they had neither cut their hair nor used chemicals or anything else to alter its texture. However, they each seemed like just another Full Gospel service so I did not continue my visits.

Concerned about seeing Jinx again, as I had taken a liking to him after the great support he had extended to mankind in times past, I visited Terry's new church, Yad-El Tabernacle. My experience that day was different. I felt as though I was the only person in the congregation and that the pastor was speaking directly to me.

He spoke of the Eagle's Story as told by the prophet William Marrion Branham, which tells of a farmer who found an egg and brought it to his barnyard, where he placed it under a mother hen to hatch with her other eggs. When this egg was hatched, the hatchling was different from the other chickens. He did not understand the hen's clucking, and his diet was different from the others'. One day his mama came hunting him, and when she saw him, she let out a scream. When he heard that scream, he realized who he was: he was an eagle, as he had been to begin with. He wasn't a chicken.

This story is a metaphor for the move from a partial realization of yourself to a more perfect understanding of who you are and what you're destined to achieve, a move that to me represented a shift from a political mindset to a spiritual mindset. I felt as though I had met God face-to-face and was coming to myself. A predestinated seed lying within me had quickened and I was flying away from the things of the world to achieve a more eternal objective.

I saw myself in the Word of God for the first time, as a part of the scripture that had come to life and as an extension of God's plan for the redemption of humankind. Most of the questions I had had over the years were being answered. I could not believe that another person on this earth was thinking like me. I vowed to return to this place at least once per month. My prior church's teachings would no longer suffice. It was like comparing elementary school with university.

After two more services at my previous place of worship, I could not continue, so I began attending Yad-El Tabernacle full time. Shortly after, I popped in to say hello to a former student of mine. It turned out that her husband had a deliverance ministry. This was my first encounter with him. His wife, being aware of some of the problems that I had been facing at the time, suggested that I ask him to pray with me. As he began to pray, I started vomiting uncontrollably. This continued for a while, until he eventually told me to come back a few days later, when he would be having a deliverance service and the anointing would be stronger. During the days that followed, I was once more filled with the peace I had experienced once before while in prison. I also had another dream.

When I attended the service on the designated day, I saw people vomiting, falling on the floor, screaming, and engaging in other types of behaviors. It was the first time that I had been to a deliverance service. A prayer line was subsequently called, which I joined. While the pastor was praying for me, I felt my head getting light, then my whole body began to vibrate uncontrollably. I could barely walk back to my seat and had to be assisted. I could not sit down. The pastor's wife eventually came and whispered in my ear that the Holy Spirit was doing work in me. She later told me that she had received a word from the Lord saying that he knew of my seeking him, he had heard my prayers, and he would reveal himself to me in three days. The pastor also disclosed that he had seen me in a dream one year prior, sitting on the same spot and looking at him from the side of the post beside which I was sitting. The room had been rearranged for the session.

The following day, I accompanied a group of orphans and children from homes in various parts of Trinidad to Tobago. My arrival there was like walking into the dream I had had the night before. The journey and the accommodation all consisted of familiar sights.

At the end of my stay, I was ready to be rebaptized in the name of the Lord Jesus Christ. Sometime before, I'd had a dream in which I was climbing a very high, steep, and rugged mountain. When I reached the plateau at the top, the mountain changed into a pyramid of glass that rose out of the sea and reflected the blue ocean below. The rain then began to pour from the heavens, falling upon me. I was jumping and shouting that the Lord was pouring holy water on me. A change came over me, and I was transported to a seat in the front pew of Yad-El Tabernacle. Pastor Terrence Thornhill was at the pulpit when I looked back and saw familiar faces in the congregation. Around that time, I used to accompany a friend, Ms. Kathleen Titus, to Morris Cerullo's crusades and had read some of his books. He was an American Pentecostal evangelist who traveled extensively around the world. When I told her of my dream, she began screaming and shouting excitedly, "Latter Rain anointing! Baptism of the Holy Ghost!"

After my return to Trinidad following the trip to Tobago, I attended service at the tabernacle on the following Sunday. On meeting a friend whom I had met in prison and not long after had invited to hear the Word as it was being preached there, I told her that I had something to tell her. She responded by saying that she also had something to tell me, and she wanted to speak first. She then disclosed that she was going to be baptized the following Saturday. I had meant to tell her that I was going to be baptized at the next baptism. We both got baptized the following Saturday.

While in the water, I was shaking and tears were rolling down my cheeks. I do not cry easily, and I was not cold.

Above: Morning of my baptism, April 1995.

I later learned that my friend had had a dream in which the world seemed to be ending, and when she ran outside her house, the sky was ablaze with the signs of the zodiac. She then began crying and begged God for a chance to get baptized and change her life.

A brother who had belonged to the guerrilla unit at Point Fortin had been a rural guerrilla in both the south and the north and had eventually been arrested, after which he spent time in prison on remand for guns and ammunition, subsequently being miraculously freed. He had converted to Christianity, and following a dream involving Jesus, in which Terrence Thornhill and I were both present, he had begun inviting me to church and had given me books on William Marrion Branham and his ministry, including *An Exposition of the Seven Church Ages*, *The Seven Seals*, and *A Man Sent from God*, as well as some of the more than one thousand two hundred sermons or messages Branham preached during his ministry, which went seven times around the world. His commission was to prepare the people for the Second Coming of Jesus Christ, just as John the Baptist had prepared them for his First Coming.

These books had been in my library for more than ten years, yet I had never before felt inspired to read them. In my ignorance, I often felt that the writer was taking too long to get to the point, and I could not understand most of what I read. Following my baptism, God's quickening power began its work in me. I began reading these books and could not get enough of them. I could not believe that I had had these treasures on my bookshelf all this time. They were just what my soul needed for this part of the journey.

The knowledge I gained from these readings changed the way I thought about the world I live in and the world beyond. The works spoke of the birth of William Marrion Branham in a log cabin in Kentucky, USA, in the year 1909. A strange light had circled the room and stopped over his crib, and a snow-white dove had landed on the window, looked at the child, and cooed when he was fifteen minutes old.

Branham saw visions from early childhood, and from about age seven, a voice used to speak to him out of a whirlwind, saying, "Do not smoke, drink, or defile your body in any way. There'll be work to do when you get older."

Among the other supernatural events that surrounded his early life was the fact that a Gypsy fortune teller once said to him that he was being followed by a light and that he was born for a divine calling. An astrologer also told him that there was a divine aura surrounding him and that he was a gift from God to humankind. An angel later appeared to him and told him, "Do not fear. I am sent from the presence of God to tell you that you were born a peculiar birth and that your peculiar life has been to indicate that you're to take the gift of divine healing to the people of the world."

In 1933, Branham preached his first sermon. While baptizing his seventeenth person in the Ohio River in Jeffersonville, Indiana, a voice told him three times to look up! When he looked up, he saw a circle of fire hanging directly overhead, and a voice said, "As John the Baptist was sent to forerun the First Coming of Jesus Christ, so were you sent with a message to forerun his Second Coming." The light swirled overhead for less than a minute. Branham went on to baptize more than two hundred candidates in the name of the Lord Jesus Christ.

Somehow William Marrion Branham knew the pasts and futures of people he had never known before. He traveled the world seven times elevating Jesus Christ and pointing people back to him. His life was an example of how a Christian should live. He demonstrated the supernatural Gospel of Jesus Christ to millions through evangelical campaigns in Europe, Africa, India, and other countries. He revolutionized the Christian world by breaking down barriers and bringing Christians together in oneness of spirit, teaching that Jesus is what he promised to be and sharing how Jesus expected his people to live, fulfilling the scripture, "And he shall turn the hearts of the fathers to the children and the hearts of the children back to the fathers" (Holy Bible – Malachi 4:6 KJV).

Branhan's message liberated people from denominational bondage and prepared them for the liberty of the Holy Spirit, which takes place in the spiritual realm. However, the spiritual precedes the natural, and therefore wars of independence and for the liberation of the oppressed around the world followed Branham's death in 1965, since he had released a spiritual anointing upon the earth. It was during this time that I became involved in revolution and NUFF, although I was unaware of this reality relating to Branham.

The books I mentioned also detail God's plan of redemption after humankind fell from grace in the Garden of Eden. William Marrion Branham's prophetic messages foretells the biblical events being fulfilled in these end times. They tell where you are going to be when your journey comes to an end and beyond the grave and rapture. They speak of seven distinct periods of Christianity that the world will go through before the end comes and the Holy Spirit leads Christians into a spirit-filled life, where they can live victoriously despite Satan's efforts to defeat them.

I realized that these books had in them the answers to all the questions I had been asking concerning my journey on this earth and the mysterious events that were unfolding around my life. Previously, I had only understood some things in part, but now the whole picture was coming into view. For me, this was the fulfillment of the scripture "But in the days of the voice of the seventh angel, when he shall begin to sound the mysteries of God should be finished, as he hath declared to his servants the prophets (Holy Bible -Revelation 10:7 KJV).

Finally, I understood my purpose on the earth, which is to showcase Christ, thereby helping to point others to him. I was now seeing the fulfillment of the promises in the Bible, which made it a real book to me. I was truly being liberated from the darkness of ignorance and from Satan's agenda, including all the traps and snares that were meant to destroy me. Being no longer entangled with the affairs of this life, I was now viewing things from a spiritual perspective. The knowledge I gained from both the books and the Bible broke the yoke of bondage and the shackles that had me bound both mentally and spiritually. I was now being truly set free.

After about three years of attending services three days per week at the tabernacle, which was a journey of approximately eighty kilometers from where I lived, I began to question whether I should continue to attend services there when there were at least three other tabernacles located closer to my home. My children were now falling back in school as a consequence, and the driving was taking a toll on me, among other things. One night I found myself desperately praying and asking God for divine direction beyond the shadow of a doubt to be given to me.

I dreamt that night that as I walked out onto the front porch of my house, which is situated on a hill, I saw in the sky an angel dressed in long flowing white robes with a golden trumpet held upright with both hands as if blowing the trumpet, but no sound was coming from it. A voice told me to go down the stairs, which I did. Emanating from the angel was a circle of light like the reflection from a searchlight on the street. I was told to step in the circle of light. When I did so, the angel began to move along with the light, which I kept walking in. People were coming out of their houses and following in awe.

From Oropouche, we walked up Mosquito Creek, up the Sir Solomon Hochoy Highway, and straight to the tabernacle at Enterprise, Chaguanas. On reaching the tabernacle, the angel entered and went and stood on the left side of the pulpit while holding the trumpet in the same upraised position. It was Communion and foot-washing night at the tabernacle. The pastor, Brother Terrence, was standing in the aisle with what resembled a treasure chest filled with little vials in front of him. I proceeded to stand next to him. He then asked me to hand him the oil. I searched among the vials and found one with a blue and white cover, which I handed to him.

At this point, a deacon came over to us asking whether Brother Terrence was sure that this was the oil. Brother Terrence replied in the affirmative, saying that this was the anointing oil. The angel then spoke for the first and only time, saying, "Eat and drink!"

I immediately woke up with the thought that the angel meant to eat the bread and drink the wine and, therefore, I should commune there. At the time I had told no one of this dream. Two weeks later, on an actual Communion night, I heard the pastor during his sermon say, "To eat and drink is to do the will of the Father in the place where he appoints you!" That settled it.

One evening not long after this, when I was on my way home from work, I stopped to chat with my friend at the home for the aged. She knew that I no longer fellowshipped at the former church since I used to drop in from time to time to discuss the scriptures and to testify of what the Lord was doing in my life. That day, after talking for a while, I remembered that it was a service day, so I informed my friend that I had to leave right away. To my surprise, she responded with, "The next time you are going to service, I would like to go with you." I asked her whether she was certain and informed her of the next service day, which was two days away. She then asked me to pass by for her. Two days later, when I arrived at her door, she was ready and waiting.

We did not sit next to each other during the service on account of the location of the empty seats. However, on our way home, I asked her what she thought of the service. Her response was, "It was good. Very good. I am feeling like the woman at the well. I was hungry and got food." I then asked her whether she would come again. She replied, "Yes, anytime."

Within a month she was baptized in the name of the Lord Jesus Christ. Some of her children and grandchildren followed. It was only after her baptism, when she gave her testimony, that I learned that during the service she felt the Holy Spirit had begun convicting her of her sins, resulting in her being bathed in tears. She said that in the days that followed she was not the same, that her life had been turned upside down and inside out with her feeling joyful, whereas she used to cry uncontrollably every day.

Following her baptism, she asked whether the pastor would keep services in the church over which she was overseer and spiritual mother as it had had twelve successive pastors with none meeting the requirements of a true pastor. The last one had abandoned the church for greener pastures abroad. I told my friend that one way of knowing would be to ask Brother Terry. It turned out that twenty-four years prior he had had a vision that a woman had given him a church. He received the confirmation that this was it.

Again, there was another dream. After practicing as a social worker for about fourteen years, I dreamt that I was attending a graduation ceremony at the University of the West Indies–Saint Augustine, Trinidad. The chancellor, whose name I could recall was George Alleyne, called my name, and when I stood to my feet, he said, "I am presenting to you your Master's," while presenting me with a Master's degree. At this point, I awoke from sleep and for days was disturbed by this dream. I had thought the possibility of my pursuing a master's degree was extremely remote, almost impossible. The thought had never crossed my mind, not that I was in any financial position to return to school. Therefore, I decided to pray and release the idea. I told God that if this dream was from him, then I would not have to worry about it. I was leaving it entirely in his hands. Three months later, I began studying for a master's degree at the University of the West Indies, Saint Augustine, Trinidad.

I was having a casual conversation with a friend I had not seen for quite a while when she disclosed that she was employed at the Prime Minister's Constituency Office. As we chatted, I indicated that I long had had a desire to extend my thanks for the scholarship that I had been granted, but since the then PM who had extended the courtesies had passed on, I never did so. It then dawned on me that Mr. Patrick Manning, then the present prime minister, would have been a part of the cabinet that had approved the scholarship and, therefore, it would be fitting to see him and express my gratitude.

My friend was instrumental in setting up the appointment. Upon my meeting Prime Minister Manning, he was taken aback that I had not come to ask for any favors, which was the norm with constituents, but was there simply to say thank you. He seemed impressed with my life after prison thus far and offered to help me in any way possible should I need any help.

I had seen a master's program advertised and applied, and was short-listed, but during the interview I could not convince the interviewers that I would be able to do a very intensive full-time course. I had met all the other requirements, but I did not have sufficient vacation leave, nor could I have afforded leave without pay. This was when Mr. Manning's offer came to the rescue.

After the successful completion of the master's degree, I returned to his office to again thank him and present him with my degree. His response was, "You know, you are more qualified than me now. I want you to go on and do your doctorate. I will personally sponsor you." Following this, he proceeded to gather his staff and others at his Constituency Office, telling them of my experience as a guerrilla in the Northern Range in the early 1970s and of my imprisonment for my part in those activities. He then referred to me as "a role model for young people," stating how proud he was of me while hugging me in a fatherly manner. This was met with continuous applause.

I did not immediately take up the prime minister's offer because my sons had reached the stage where I felt that I should step back and let them attend university. So, I politely demurred, telling him that I would give it some consideration. His response was that I should get back to him as soon as I was ready. Not long after, he demitted from office. His health began to decline, and he subsequently passed on. God rest his soul.

I was now on fire for the Lord more than ever before. I could not hold a conversation without gravitating back to the Word. I began seeing God in everyone and everything. He is now everything to me. He is the only way, the only truth, and the only real life. Jesus is the answer for the world today since the only true answer for a better human coexistence is a return to the principles of God. I could not get enough of the Message of the Hour as expounded by the God-sent vindicated prophet for this Laodicean Age, William Marrion Branham. All the mysteries in the Word were now being revealed to me.

The course that my life took and the outcome, I now see all of it as part of God's plan of redemption. Since he is the Source of all things, true power comes from him. Only he can provide the answers and give the peace, love, and joy needed to navigate the challenges of this life.

It is my firm belief that "all things work together for good to them that love God, to them who are the called according to his purpose." (Holy Bible -Romans 8:28 KJV). He takes us through different paths to fulfill his purpose for our lives. This has been my experience through the years. We only need to trust him and have faith in his Word.

I have found the answers to the myriad questions that I had and even more via the message of the prophet and the Word of God. I now know who I am in Christ Jesus and I am preparing for his coming, when "the dead in Christ shall rise first. Then we which are alive and remain shall be caught up together with them in the clouds to meet the Lord in the air: and so shall we ever be with the Lord" (Holy Bible -Thessalonians 4:16-17 KJV).

It is no longer a natural battle, but a spiritual one. The world has become so dark that you cannot see unless the light of the world, which is Christ, is in you. "For we wrestle not against flesh and blood, but against principalities, against powers, against the rulers of the darkness of this world, against spiritual wickedness in high places" (Holy Bible - Ephesians 5:12 KJV).

It would take another book to tell of Christ's love and grace in my life and of his work among the people.

THE ANSWER

The only answer to war is the spiritualization of the minds of men. The answers to the problems that confront us as individuals, and as one world, can only come through an awakening of the spiritual nature of man.

—May Roland, *Dare to Believe*

EPILOGUE

Terrence Thornhill is still a minister of the gospel, having aborted his studies at the Catholic University of America during his quest for truth, before becoming a freedom fighter.

Jennifer Jones entered conventional politics and became a senator and then Minister of Government after obtaining a degree in agriculture at the University of the West Indies–Saint Augustine, Trinidad. She also became a Cuban-trained vet and subsequently went on to serve a term as Trinidad and Tobago's ambassador to Cuba.

Clyde Haynes, who was initially employed as a molder in a factory that made kitchen utensils, including pots, pans, and coal pots, had successfully pursued General Certificate Exams at both ordinary and advanced levels while in prison. Following his release, he obtained a BSc degree in economics. He was given a presidential pardon by President Maxwell Richards after becoming coordinator of the Prisons Education Program, which included Carrera Prison, Golden Grove male and female prisons, and the Youth Training Center. In 1990, he started his own organization, the National Academy of Business Arts and Computing.

Andrea Jacob became a professional social worker after obtaining both a BSc and a master's degree in social work at the University of the West Indies–Mona campus, Jamaica, and Saint Augustine campus, Trinidad and Tobago, respectively. She was employed as a medical social worker in the Health Services of Trinidad and Tobago for approximately thirty years. She also pursued drug and addiction studies at the University of the Virgin Islands–Saint Thomas and is an Internationally Certified Employee Assistance Professional.

APPENDIX

PROPAGANDA

The foreign investors, through their local agents, the Williams government, the police force, and local big businesses, are presently bringing off endless rope against the people.

We have only to notice the skyrocketing cost of living, widespread unemployment, increasing acts of violence by the police (especially against the most scrutinizing elements), and the continued exploitation of our labor to realize this.

Our society continues to remain organized to serve the interests of the privileged few rather than to bring benefits to the majority of our people. The foreign investor is the big man in this setup and is present in the form of the oil companies, for example, Amoco and Texaco; the banks (Barclays, Nova Scotia); big industry (Neal and Massey, Dunlop); the insurance firms (American Life); and all major areas of distribution.

The foreign investor's aim is and has always been to rob and exploit, and he has been at this for centuries.

The continuous resistance to this foreign oppression that our people have always waged from the days of chattel slavery has, however, forced this bandit to modify his methods somewhat. It was the workers' struggle led by Butler in the 1937–39 period that wrung from the hands of the man whatever minor concessions (e.g., 1962 independence) granted us at present.

The man has always been careful, however, to retain control over the most important aspect of our lives: production. Realizing that direct exploitation could endanger his position of dominance, the man has created a special class of local exploiters consisting of government officials and big local capitalists whose task is to manage the political, social, and cultural methods of exploitation that have replaced direct exploitation.

The rope arm of the man's group of oppressors is the police force. Our attempts to effect the changes denied us in the years following 1962 in the past, by largely peaceful means, were met with ruthless suppression, injury, and death. Since then, the state-run machinery has been misled, and a specialized antipeople force (the SSS) has been developed. The brutality of the SSS has been perfected and openly tested as evidenced by the James Brown incident in February 1972; the Pele incident in September 1972; and more lately the western-style execution of a scrutinizing citizen at Saint Ann's in January 1973.

Dr. Williams has come out in Parliament and openly supported the action of his rope men, so we can expect these acts to continue and increase in the future. Our actions today are to direct our people's struggle against foreign domination to new heights and to lead it to the final and total overthrow of the foreigner and his local stooges.

We anticipate endless distress for the people if things continue as they are, and we understand that there can be no solution to any of our problems while the important areas of our lives are controlled from abroad. We also understand that the only way to stand up against and defeat the violence of the oppressing minority is for the people to engage in even greater violence. The man and his local agents will brand our actions as banditry and us as bandits because we have attacked him and relieved him of some of the wealth that rightfully belongs to the people.

In the hands of the people, it will be used to strengthen and spread armed resistance to achieve total liberation from foreign exploitation. Our roots lie deep among the most oppressed groups of our people (workers, the unemployed, farmers, students, housewives), and nothing the man does will prevent his final overthrow.

We have learned well from our 1970 experiences. The selflessness and dedication of our fighters points to the existence of a new type of individual who is prepared, as Brother Hillary Valentine and Brother Joel de Masia were, to die to achieve true liberation.

We call on all popular progressive organizations in our society to unite so that we can rally the broadest possible force to intensify the people's armed resistance. There can be no other strategy! Our armed resistance is to support and strengthen all present areas of struggle by the people: the struggle of the workers in general against the exploitation by foreigners, and particularly the struggle of the workers in the oil industry against the threatened CIA destruction of their union; the struggle of the farmers throughout the country, and particularly those in the Sugar Belt against Tate and Lyle Williams's oppression; the struggle of the unemployed and underemployed against the all-out efforts of the man to deprive them of the right to live; and the struggles of the housewives and children against daily hardships.

Further, we support all struggles of oppressed peoples throughout the world, particularly those being waged by our Caribbean brothers and sisters. True Caribbean unity is a necessity and will only be achieved through the collective armed resistance of the people in the region against the divide-and-rule strategy of the foreign exploiters.

We are one people. The enemy now appears big and strong, and the armed resistance of the people is small and weak, but by taking advantage of the enemy's weaknesses, the armed resistance of the people will expand and grow strong.

The final victory will belong to the people.

National United Freedom Fighters

PEOPLE'S FREEDOM COMMITTEE

THE TRUTH

about

N.U.F.F.

DECLARATION

Recently, the People's Freedom Committee was formed. It was formed with four specific aims which are as follows :—

(1) that all Political Prisoners be immediately set free;

(2) that the barbarous system of Capital Punishment that still exists in this 'civilised' country be abolished;

(3) that immediate and urgent steps be taken to eliminate the sub-human conditions prevailing in the country's prisons;

(4) that the laws guaranteeing the democratic rights and freedoms of the citizens be strictly adhered to particularly with respect to violent acts of police intimidation, unjustifiable arrest and detention, the denial of access to legal counsel, excessive bail, illegal entry and trumped-up charges.

The formation of this Committee must not be viewed as accidental, but must be seen as an inevitable part of the overall objective development of the people's struggle against all forms of exploitation and oppression as perpetrated by the ruling class of Trinidad and Tobago.

This is clearly seen in its aims particularly in relation to the struggle for the release of political prisoners and the infringement on the democratic rights of the citizens. Both these phenomena must be seen within the context of the development of the struggle against oppression.

1971 saw the beginning of the armed phase of the struggle in Trinidad and Tobago, the vanguard being the National United Freedom Fighters. This struggle is political in nature. However, from their inception the bourgeois press has waged a consistent propaganda campaign against NUFF, labelling them a bunch of common criminals, and their activities as acts of banditry.

This campaign, along with the limited circulation of the organisation's propaganda has created a situation of ignorance by the public about the nature of the organisation, and of its objectives.

Recognising this fact, the People's Freedom Committee as part of its campaign is presenting a position paper by the National United Freedom Fighters. This paper has several aims in mind, but particularly the following:—

(1) tracing the development and nature of the organisation;

(2) establishing the fact that its imprisoned members are political prisoners and not common criminals;

(3) organising support not only for the release of the political prisoners but for the achievement of the other aims of the People's Freedom Committee as well.

The history of the Commonwealth Caribbean has been one of exploitation of its inhabitants and resources by foreign agents. In this regard, one can clearly see three distinct periods during which our people have been used by three different types of systems.

First, there is the 200-odd years (1623—1838) of colonization in which slave labour was used to finance the Industrial Revolution and, as a result, the rise of the capitalist class of Britain

Secondly, there is the period of increasing Crown Colony rule (1838—1944) under which the emancipated slaves and their descendants and working class successors laboured on plantations under the most oppressive conditions. This was partly due to the abandonment of the planter class of the W.I. by Britain who no longer found it profitable to purchase sugar from the West Indian monopolists.

Thirdly, the period of 1944 to the present time, during which the Trade Union movement evolved, along with adult suffrage (the right to vote), and political independence, without any real change in the economic repression which is constant throughout our history.

In the period 1934—38, due to a disastrous drop in the price of sugar, there was massive un-employment, food shortages, strikes and riots throughout the Caribbean. In St. Kitts, Trinidad, Jamaica and other islands, the people showed their anger and discontent in no uncertain terms. Leaders, most of them middle class, who were able to catch the imagination of the people evolved and became spokesmen of the popular movements for change.

From those movements the trade unions were formed, and then the political parties. Such leaders included Grantley Adams of Barbados, Bustamante and Manley of Jamaica, and Cipriani and Butler of Trinidad. It was after this militant period, which was investigated by various commissions and study groups sent by Britain, that the right of the West Indian islands to self-government was grudgingly recognised by Britain.

Around this time, too, the idea of Federation as the vehicle for Independence, was proposed. This didn't work, however, and subsequently various islands separately attained their political independence, but with no real change in their economic dependence on the imperialist countries. It is against this background that the present struggle against imperialism in all its new forms must be viewed in order to get a clearer picture of the continuity of the fight for political and economic freedom.

1   Here, in Trinidad in 1969, the workers' struggle against the injustice of capitalist corporation again came into the forefront with the historic bus-strike after which over two hundred workers, in addition to being brutally beaten, were dismissed from their jobs. This was the start of another period of labour unrest which to today is still continuing.

In 1970 a State of Emergency was declared and trade union leaders, members of the National Joint Action Committee, as well as other activists were detained. This was done with the sole intention of suppressing the people's legitimate claim for the right to control their own political, economic and cultural destiny. The capitalist - based Williams regime made a desperate effort to pass the Public Order Bill, which was in effect, a cleverly construed document geared to rape the working class people of their most fundamental rights, and to stifle the people's protests against the imperial system.

However, due to a barrage of protests from different groups representing almost the entire cross-section of the population, the proposed Bill was thrown out. The regime was not to be outdone, however, and it skilfully prepared and passed separate bills, as for example, the Firearms Act, the Summary Offences Act, the Sedition Act, Industrial Relations Act, all of which were really Acts enforcing the clauses of the rejected Public Order Bill. These Acts were passed in the most repressive atmosphere of another State of Emergency, and were designed in general to infringe upon the rights of all working class people.

Also, during 1970, brutality by the police was rampant and so were their methods of armed terrorism. Large sums of taxpayers' money were spent on the acquisition of automatic rifles and sub-machine guns and on the imprisonment and trial of the soldiers against the will of the people.

It was now quite clear that War had been declared against the people. Expertly coached and equipped by the C.I.A. the regime engaged in a deliberate and systematic campaign designed to frustrate, imprison and liquidate the hard-core protesting elements in the country. The houses of known militant leaders and others were searched and plundered time and time again, and the police maintained a relentless form of harrassment against the peacefully resisting population. The blocks were singled out as the prime area of operation for this oppressive and anti-revolutionary campaign. Brothers peacefully gathering on blocks discussing the state of the country were constantly raided by robot-like policemen. Many were taken away, questioned, beaten, threatened and released; others were beaten and framed on charges ranging from possession of marijuana, and arms and ammunition, to shooting with intent. Still others were tortured into turning informers, and others not so fortunate were shot and wounded, sometimes killed.

Because of the frequency and precision with which these "Block Raids" were carried out, brothers and sisters realised that these illegal raids were a means by which the decaying political regime was seeking to rid itself of meaningful opposition and to maintain itself in power. Taking this into consideration, brothers on the blocks decided that they would have to protect themselves from further victimisation at the hands of the notorious "Frame Squad", and to adopt a more militant form of resistance in the face of the ever present brutality of the police.

Given the unemployment, the intimidation and the depressing conditions of existence experienced by young people throughout the country, the wonder is that an organisation like N.U.F.F. did not emerge sooner. The more conscious brothers began to organise themselves, and decided on certain lines of political activity. And so, under the above mentioned repressive conditions, the National United Freedom Fighters was born.

N.U.F.F. is an organisation comprised of young men and women with the average age of twenty two (22). The organisation took its stand to commit itself to armed struggle after it realised that talk alone would not bring us the required living conditions for which our people have been clamouring. N.U.F.F. realised that the solution to the situation here in Trinidad and Tobago, and in the world in general does not lie in higher wages, or even in the attainment of a high standard of living for everyone. In other words, change on the physical (material) level alone would not necessarily result in a progressive society. If we were to have a house food and clothing to suit our every need, and the base, corrupt instincts and inclinations in man such as lust, greed and corruption remain uncurbed, then the resulting society would still be doomed.

Hence a lifestyle based on the development of our dormant spiritual and moral consciousness is inevitable. A lifestyle that does away with imperialism and capitalism and replaces these two evils with socialism, is also inevitable.

It should be noted that N.U.F.F. is saying that a revolution of the mind is on and should progress hand in hand with the socialist, economic, political, cultural and industrial revolution. This present generation is being called upon to make a world-wide sacrifice, so that future generations would meet improved living conditions on this planet.

Teachings on the Self, on the ultimate purpose of man, on moral conduct etc, should be encouraged and carried out at all levels, in the house, in the schools, and among the broad mass of the population. Contrary to the beliefs of most people, these teachings are not to be considered as separate from education along economic, political, cultural, technical and industrial lines. People need to be educated at all levels, so that well-balanced individuals would develop and a well-balanced progressive society would result. This progress of attaining knowledge is essential for the realisation of Self and for living in harmony with each other and with the Absolute (God). These are necessary prerequisites for the establishment of a successful revolutionary and progressive society.

During its period of activity, thirteen members of N.U.F.F. were killed in action against the state forces. Those were :— Hilary Valentine 1/7/72 at Arima; Adolph De Masia 29/7/72 at Lopinot, Ulric Gransaul, Mervyn Andrews, John Beddoe and Nathaniel Jack 22/2/73 at Laventille, Kenneth Tenia and Beverley Jones 13/9/73 at Caura, Guy Harewood 17/10/73 at Curepe, Brian Jeffers and Dexter Assing 3/12/73 at St. James, Rance Madhoo 9/12/73 at Pt. Fortin, and Ray Ransome 22/12/73 at San Fernando.

Members of the organisation who were fortunate enough not to be gunned down, and are in prison are Michael Lewis, Andy Thomas, Kirkland Paul, Bunny Gransaul, Anthony Alexander, Peter Chandree, Lennox Daniel and Winston Ferreira Those who were able to meet the excessive bails set by the relevant legal authorities are :— Trevor Bowen, Rudolph Hernandez, Terrence Thornhill, Jennifer Jones, Malcolm Kernahan, Alan Harewood. Others, like Andre Jacob and Clyde Haynes, have already been convicted, and are currently serving sentences.

CASE OF DAVID MICHAEL

Above: David Michael in 1973.

David Michael was brutally beaten and framed for the murder of a policeman. His trial was highlighted by overt lying on the part of the police, prejudiced statements on the part of the judge, and unusual and unwarranted pressure on the jury to secure a conviction. Convicted on September 24, 1974, he spent a year on death row at Royal Goal, where he embarked on a fourteen-day hunger strike in protest against authorities' tactical denial of his rights to properly prepare himself for his appeal. This was done by delaying the copy of the judge's summation and refusing David Michael access to a specific law journal. His protest was against psychological pressures and prison conditions in general. He had several times been brought to the gallows and told by his tormentors to take a good look at what was in store for him. Following a retrial, he was eventually freed in May 1977.

Members of NUFF who were killed during the early 1970s.

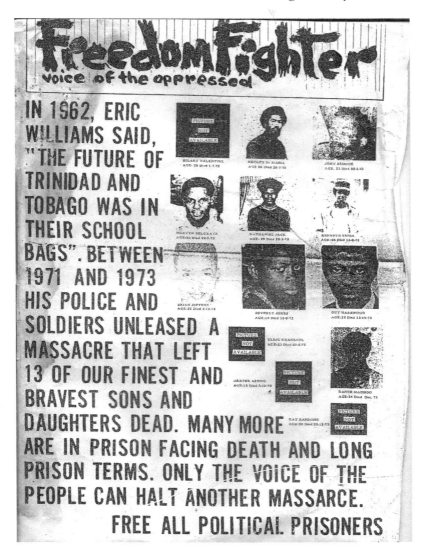

FREEDOM FIGHTER? YES. CRIMINAL? NO.

In March of 1975, a comrade was placed on trial at the high court. He was charged with possession of a firearm, kidnapping, and robbery with aggravation in a seven-count indictment. During the trial, the comrade, who was unrepresented by counsel, thoroughly shattered the prosecution's case. The witnesses were thoroughly entangled in their conflicting and inconsistent evidence. The jury, who returned after fifteen minutes, returned a verdict of not guilty on all counts. The judge was very surprised and displeased with the verdict. The jury, however, had been strongly influenced by the fact that the comrade was able to show them and the public that he was being prosecuted for political actions and that he was a political prisoner.

Before dismissing the jury, the judge asked a policeman for the comrade's notes of evidence. It appears that the police had told the judge that the comrade had subversive writings on the back of his notes of evidence. What he had written was, "Freedom fighter: yes. Criminal: no."

The judge then asked the comrade if he had anything to say as to why he should not be jailed for contempt of court. As the comrade started to put his matter in a political context, he was promptly silenced by the judge, who then sentenced him to three months in prison. He was further denied the right to appeal this sentence.

William Marrion Branham, 1950.

Michael Als, 1976.

Made in the USA
Middletown, DE
28 September 2024

61526558R00102